INTEGRATING SCIENCE 1–2 with Reading Instruction

12 Complete Science Units

Written by
Trisha Callella and Marilyn Marks

Editor: LaDawn Walter
Illustrator: Catherine Rader
Cover Illustrator: Rick Grayson
Designer: Moonhee Pak
Cover Designer: Moonhee Pak
Art Director: Tom Cochrane
Project Director: Carolea Williams

Table of Contents

Introduction

For many children, reading comprehension diminishes when they read nonfiction text. Children often have difficulty understanding scientific vocabulary, making inferences, and grasping scientific concepts. With so much curriculum to cover each day, science is sometimes put on the back burner when it comes to academic priorities. *Integrating Science with Reading Instruction 1–2* provides the perfect integration of science content with specific reading instruction to help children improve their comprehension of nonfiction text and maximize every minute of your teaching day.

This resource includes twelve units that cover three areas of science—life, earth, and physical. The units are based on the most common science topics taught in grades 1–2 in accordance with the National Science Education Standards:

Life Science	**Earth Science**	**Physical Science**
In the Sea	Rocks	Matter
On the Farm	The Sun	Simple Machines
The Zoo	Clouds	Magnets
Life Cycles	Stormy Weather	Shadows

Each unit includes powerful prereading strategies, such as predicting what the story will be about, accessing prior knowledge, and brainstorming about vocabulary that may be included in the reading selection. Following the prereading exercises is a nonfiction reading selection written on a grade 1–2 reading level. Each reading selection is followed by essential postreading activities such as comprehension questions on multiple taxonomy levels, skill reviews, and a critical thinking exercise. Each unit also includes a hands-on science experiment that follows the scientific method. The descriptions on pages 5–8 include the objectives and implementation strategies for each unit component.

Before, during, and after reading the story, children are exposed to the same reading strategies you typically reinforce during your language arts instruction block. This powerful duo gives you the opportunity to teach both reading and science simultaneously. Using the activities in this resource, children will continue *learning to read* while *reading to learn.* They will become more successful readers while gaining new science knowledge and experiences.

Prereading Strategies
- ✓ Catch a Clue
- ✓ Concept Map
- ✓ Word Warm-Up

↓

Nonfiction Text

↓

Postreading Applications
- ✓ Comprehension Questions
- ✓ Sharpen Your Skills
- ✓ Get Logical

↓

Hands-on Science

Connections to Standards

This chart shows the National Science Education Standards that are covered in each unit.

LIFE SCIENCE	In the Sea	On the Farm	The Zoo	Life Cycles
Organisms have basic needs.	•	•	•	•
The world has many different environments.	•	•	•	
Distinct environments support life of different organisms.	•	•	•	
Organisms can only survive where their needs are met.	•		•	
Each plant or animal has different structures that serve different functions.	•	•	•	•
Plants and animals have predictable life cycles.				•

EARTH SCIENCE	Rocks	The Sun	Clouds	Stormy Weather
Earth materials include solid rocks and soils, water, and the gases of the atmosphere.	•		•	•
Earth materials have different physical and chemical properties.	•	•	•	•
Earth materials provide many resources humans use.	•			
Objects in the sky all have properties, locations, and movements that can be observed and described.		•	•	•
The sun provides the light and heat to maintain the temperature of the earth.		•		
Weather changes from day to day and over the seasons.		•	•	•
Objects in the sky have patterns of movement.		•	•	

PHYSICAL SCIENCE	Matter	Simple Machines	Magnets	Shadows
Objects have many observable properties (e.g., size, weight, shape, color, temperature) that can be measured.	•	•	•	•
Objects are made of one or more materials (e.g., wood, metal, paper).	•	•	•	
Materials can exist in different states.	•			
Some materials can change from one state to another by heating or cooling.	•			
Light can be reflected, refracted, or absorbed by an object.				•
Magnets attract and repel each other and some other kinds of materials.			•	

Unit Overview

Prereading Strategies

Catch a Clue

Objectives

Children will

✓ be introduced to key concepts and vocabulary *before* reading
✓ be able to transfer this key strategy to improve test-taking skills

Implementation

Children will use clues and the process of elimination to predict what the nonfiction reading selection will be about. Copy this page on an overhead transparency, and use it for a whole-class activity. Begin by reading aloud each word, and ask children to repeat the words. Read the clues one at a time. Then, discuss with the class what topic(s) could be eliminated and the reasons why. (Note: There will be clues that do not eliminate any topics. The purpose of this is to teach children that although there is information listed, it is not always helpful information.) Cross off a topic when the class decides that it does not fit the clues. If there is more than one topic left after the class discusses all of the clues, this becomes a prediction activity. When this occurs, reread the clues with the class, and discuss which answer would be most appropriate given the clues provided.

Concept Map

Objectives

Children will

✓ access prior knowledge by brainstorming what they already know about the topic
✓ increase familiarity with the science content by hearing others' prior knowledge experiences
✓ revisit the map *after* reading to recall information from the reading selection

Implementation

Copy this page on an overhead transparency, and use it for a whole-class activity. Use a colored pen to write children's prior knowledge on the transparency. After the class reads the story, use a different colored pen to add what children learned.

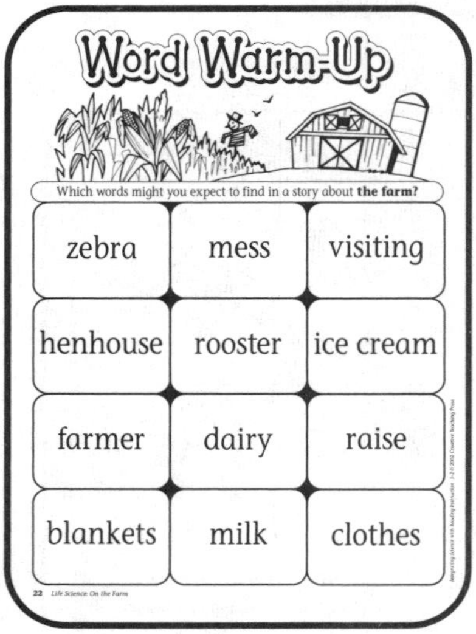

Word Warm-Up

Which words might you expect to find in a story about **the farm?**

zebra	mess	visiting
henhouse	rooster	ice cream
farmer	dairy	raise
blankets	milk	clothes

Word Warm-Up

Objectives

Children will

- ✓ be introduced to new vocabulary words
- ✓ make predictions about the story using thinking and reasoning skills
- ✓ begin to monitor their own comprehension

Implementation

Children will use the strategy of exclusion brainstorming to identify which words are likely to be in the story and which words are unrelated and should be eliminated from the list. Copy this page on an overhead transparency, and use it for a whole-class activity. Have children make predictions about which of the vocabulary words could be in the story and which words probably would not be in the story. Ask them to give reasons for their predictions. For example, say *Do you think a zebra would be at a farm?* A child may say *Yes, because it is an animal* or *No, because it is an animal that lives in the wild.* Circle the word if a child says that it will be in the story, and cross it out if a child says it will not be in the story. Do not correct children's responses. After reading, children can either confirm or disconfirm their own predictions. It is more powerful for children to verify their predictions on their own than to be told the answer before ever reading the story.

Nonfiction Text

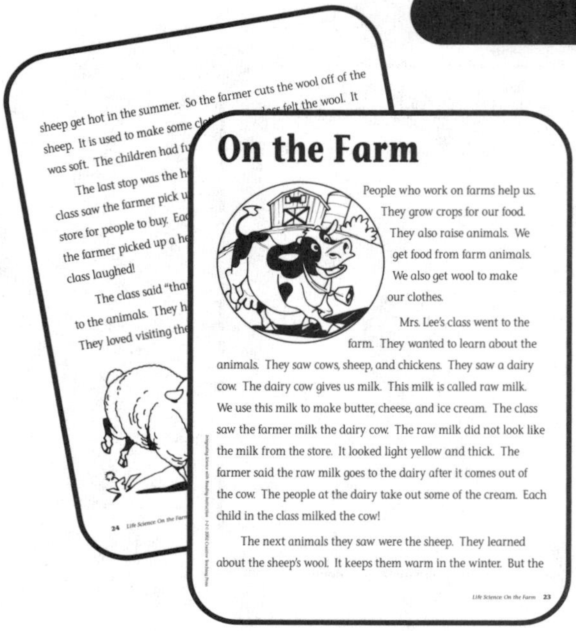

On the Farm

People who work on farms help us. They grow crops for our food. They also raise animals. We get food from farm animals. We also get wool to make our clothes.

Mrs. Lee's class went to the farm. They wanted to learn about the animals. They saw cows, sheep, and chickens. They saw a dairy cow. The dairy cow gives us milk. This milk is called raw milk. We use this milk to make butter, cheese, and ice cream. The class saw the farmer milk the dairy cow. The raw milk did not look like the milk from the store. It looked light yellow and thick. The farmer said the raw milk goes to the dairy after it comes out of the cow. The people at the dairy take out some of the cream. Each child in the class milked the cow!

The next animals they saw were the sheep. They learned about the sheep's wool. It keeps them warm in the winter. But the

The Story

Objectives

Children will

- ✓ read high-interest, nonfiction stories
- ✓ increase science knowledge
- ✓ increase content area vocabulary
- ✓ make connections between the science facts and their own experiences

Implementation

Give each student a copy of the story, and display the corresponding Word Warm-Up transparency while you read the story with the class. After the class reads the story, go back to the transparency, and have children discuss their predictions in relation to the new information they learned in the story. Invite children to identify any changes they would make on the transparency and give reasons for their responses. Then, revisit the corresponding Concept Map transparency, and write the new information children have learned.

Postreading Applications

Comprehension Questions

Objectives

Children will

✓ recall factual information

✓ be challenged to think beyond the story facts to make inferences

✓ connect the story to other reading, their own lives, and the world around them

Implementation

Use these questions to facilitate a class discussion of the story. Choose the number and types of questions that best meet the abilities of your class.

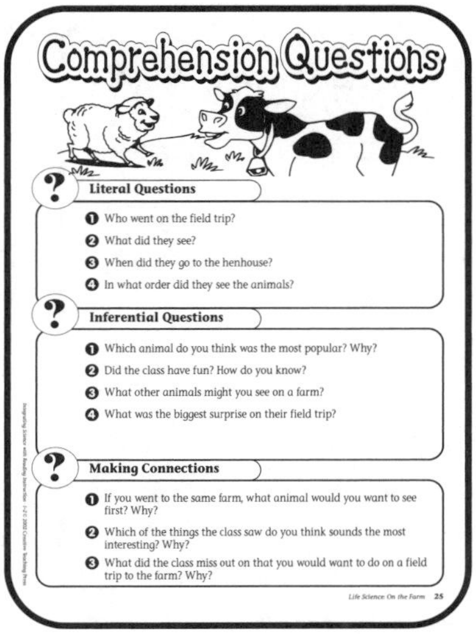
Comprehension Questions

Literal Questions

1. Who went on the field trip?
2. What did they see?
3. When did they go to the henhouse?
4. In what order did they see the animals?

Inferential Questions

1. Which animal do you think was the most popular? Why?
2. Did the class have fun? How do you know?
3. What other animals might you see on a farm?
4. What was the biggest surprise on their field trip?

Making Connections

1. If you went to the same farm, what animal would you want to see first? Why?
2. Which of the things the class saw do you think sounds the most interesting? Why?
3. What did the class miss out on that you would want to do on a field trip to the farm? Why?

Life Science On the Farm 25

Sharpen Your Skills

Objectives

Children will

✓ practice answering questions in common test-taking formats

✓ integrate language arts skills with science knowledge

Implementation

After the class reads a story, give each child a copy of this page. Ask children to read a question and all of the answer choices for that question before deciding on an answer. Show them how to use their pencil to completely fill in the circle for their answer. Invite children to raise their hand if they have difficulty reading a question and/or the answer choices. Thoroughly explain the types of questions and exactly what is being asked the first few times children use this reproducible.

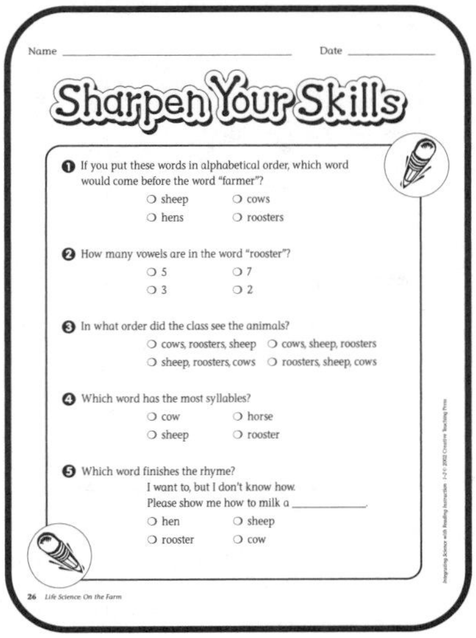
Name ______________________ Date __________

Sharpen Your Skills

1. If you put these words in alphabetical order, which word would come before the word "farmer"?
   - ○ sheep ○ cows
   - ○ hens ○ roosters
2. How many vowels are in the word "rooster"?
   - ○ 5 ○ 7
   - ○ 3 ○ 2
3. In what order did the class see the animals?
   - ○ cows, roosters, sheep ○ cows, sheep, roosters
   - ○ sheep, roosters, cows ○ roosters, sheep, cows
4. Which word has the most syllables?
   - ○ cow ○ horse
   - ○ sheep ○ rooster
5. Which word finishes the rhyme?
   I want to, but I don't know how.
   Please show me how to milk a __________.
   - ○ hen ○ sheep
   - ○ rooster ○ cow

26 Life Science On the Farm

Name ______________ Date ______

Get Logical

Carlos, Jan, and Trenton were in Mrs. Lee's class. Each child had a favorite animal from the farm. Use the clues below to decide which animal at the farm was each child's favorite.

Clues

1. Trenton's animal was soft and wooly.
2. Jan squirted her friends with this animal!
3. Carlos's animal flew out of his hands.

Cow			
Sheep			
Rooster			
	Carlos	Jan	Trenton

Carlos liked the ______________ the best.

Jan liked the ______________ the best.

Trenton liked the ______________ the best.

Life Science: On the Farm 27

Get Logical

Objectives

Children will

✓ practice logical and strategic thinking skills

✓ practice the skill of process of elimination

✓ transfer the information read by applying it to new situations

Implementation

Give each child a copy of this page. Read the beginning sentences and the clues to familiarize children with the words. Show children step-by-step how to eliminate choices based on the clues given. Have children place an X in a box that represents an impossible choice, thereby narrowing down the options for accurate choices. Once children understand the concept, they can work independently on this reproducible.

Hands-on Science

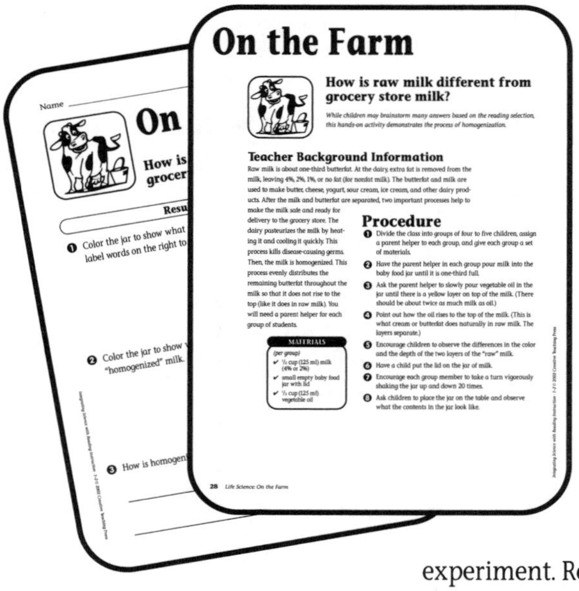

On the Farm

How is raw milk different from grocery store milk?

While children may brainstorm many answers based on the reading selection, this hands-on activity demonstrates the process of homogenization.

Teacher Background Information

Raw milk is about one-third butterfat. At the dairy, extra fat is removed from the milk, leaving 4%, 2%, 1%, or no fat (for nonfat milk). The butterfat and milk are used to make butter, cheese, yogurt, sour cream, ice cream, and other dairy products. After the milk and butterfat are separated, two important processes help to make the milk safe and ready for delivery to the grocery store. The dairy pasteurizes the milk by heating it and cooling it quickly. This process kills disease-causing germs. Then, the milk is homogenized. This process evenly distributes the remaining butterfat throughout the milk so that it does not rise to the top (like it does in raw milk). You will need a parent helper for each group of students.

MATERIALS

(per group)

✓ 1/2 cup (125 ml) milk (4% or 2%)

✓ small empty baby food jar with lid

✓ 1/2 cup (125 ml) vegetable oil

Procedure

1. Divide the class into groups of four to five children, assign a parent helper to each group, and give each group a set of materials.
2. Have the parent helper in each group pour milk into the baby food jar until it is one-third full.
3. Ask the parent helper to slowly pour vegetable oil in the jar until there is a yellow layer on top of the milk. (There should be about twice as much milk as oil.)
4. Point out how the oil rises to the top of the milk. (This is what cream or butterfat does naturally in raw milk. The layers separate.)
5. Encourage children to observe the differences in the color and the depth of the two layers of the "raw" milk.
6. Have a child put the lid on the jar of milk.
7. Encourage each group member to take a turn vigorously shaking the jar up and down 20 times.
8. Ask children to place the jar on the table and observe what the contents in the jar look like.

28 Life Science: On the Farm

Science Experiment

Objectives

Children will

✓ participate in hands-on learning experiences

✓ apply the scientific method

✓ expand and reinforce science knowledge

✓ apply new science vocabulary words

Implementation

Each experiment begins with a scientific question. Encourage children to brainstorm answers (hypotheses) and discuss their ideas based on facts they learned from the reading selection. (Additional teacher background information is provided to enhance discussions.) Help children focus on the idea that most relates to the upcoming experiment. Review the step-by-step procedure for the hands-on experiment with the class, and provide them with the necessary materials for the activity. Give each child a copy of the corresponding reproducible that uses the steps of the scientific method. Then, reread the directions step-by-step while children complete the experiment. Discuss the questions in the Results and Conclusions section, and have children write their answers on their page. The final question in this section restates the inquiry used to start the activity.

Unit Time Line

Allowing children time to reread a story several times is vital to their comprehension of the material, especially when it is nonfiction text. The following time line demonstrates how to incorporate rereading a story several times while completing all of that unit's activities as well. Use the time line as a guide to complete each unit over a week's time period.

Monday	✓ Catch a Clue (5–8 minutes) ✓ Concept Map (5–8 minutes) ✓ Word Warm-Up (5–8 minutes) ✓ Read the story with the whole class
Tuesday	✓ Reread the story in small groups ✓ Discuss some of the comprehension questions
Wednesday	✓ Reread the story with a buddy ✓ Complete Sharpen Your Skills page
Thursday	✓ Complete Get Logical page
Friday	✓ Explain teacher background information ✓ Complete hands-on science experiment

Catch a Clue

What will we learn about in our reading today?

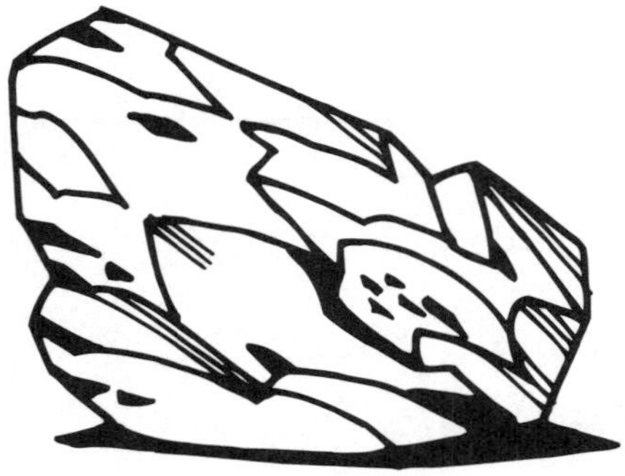

minerals

sea animals

cactus

plants

Our Clues

1. **They are living things.**
2. **They breathe, grow, and need water.**
3. **They do not grow from seeds.**

Concept Map

Facts we already know about **the sea,** and the new facts we have learned

Word Warm-Up

Which words might you expect to find in a story about **the sea?**

blubber	breathe	water
letter	school	dolphin
smart	blowhole	fluke
gills	horse	seaweed

In the Sea

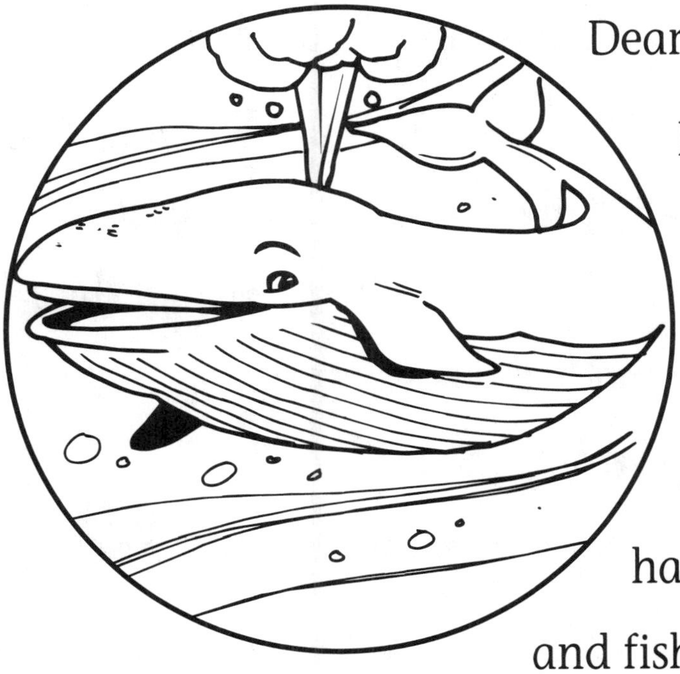

Dear Grandma,

I just read your letter. It sounds like you had fun whale watching. I hope that I can do that also. In my class, we are learning about sea life. I have learned a lot about whales and fish that live in the sea.

Did you know that whales are not fish? They are mammals. I learned that they have lungs. They also have a blowhole on the top of their head. This is how they breathe. Did you know that they swim by moving their tail fluke up and down? This helps them get to the top of the water. It also helps them dive in the sea. Large whales, like the blue or gray whales, do not have any teeth. They have rows and rows of baleen. It looks like a giant toothbrush! All whales have fat under their skin called blubber. This helps to keep them warm.

Did you see fish on your trip? In school we learned that fish come in a lot of shapes and sizes. Some are long. Some are skinny. Some are flat like a pancake. Some look like a long tube. Did you know that fish do not have lungs like whales? All fish have gills. The gills help them breathe under the water. I learned that fish move in a different way than whales. Fish swim by moving their tail fin. They move it from side to side. They use their other fins to help them steer. Did you know the sea horse cannot swim well?

I hope we can go whale watching together. I think I am ready. I have learned a lot about whales and fish in school. I would love to see the sea life I have learned about! Please write me back. I would love to see any pictures you have. I love you!

Love,

Max

Comprehension Questions

Literal Questions

1. Who went whale watching?
2. What is Max learning about in school?
3. What did Max learn about whales?
4. What did Max learn about fish?

Inferential Questions

1. Why do you think a fish's tail moves differently than a whale's tail?
2. Why do you think a whale's blowhole is on top of its head?
3. Which animal do you think could eat bigger things—a fish or a gray whale? Why?
4. What shape do you think a fast-swimming fish would be? Why?

Making Connections

1. Which sea animal would you most like to see? Why?
2. Which animal do you think is most like us—a fish or a whale? Why?
3. What part of a whale is like your nose? Why?

Name ______________________ Date ______________

Sharpen Your Skills

1 If you put these words in alphabetical order, which word would come after the word "sea horse"?

❍ dolphin ❍ bullhead shark
❍ fish ❍ sea star

2 What do large whales have in place of teeth?

❍ gums ❍ baleen
❍ blowhole ❍ fins

3 What is the action word (verb) in the following sentence?

Max learned about sea animals.

❍ about ❍ sea
❍ Max ❍ learned

4 Which word best fits this sentence?

Bullhead sharks eat crabs and shellfish by ______________ them up with their strong teeth.

❍ grind ❍ grinds
❍ grinded ❍ grinding

5 Which word would finish this analogy?

Dolphin is to **swim** like ______________ is to **crawl.**

❍ octopus ❍ whale
❍ crab ❍ seagull

Name ______________________ Date ____________

Get Logical

Tyler, Rebecca, and Sam decided to write reports on their favorite sea animal. Use the clues below to decide which animal each friend learned about.

Clues

1. Sam learned that his sea animal uses gills to breathe.
2. Tyler's animal cannot swim well.
3. Rebecca's animal has blubber under its skin.

Blue Whale			
Sea Horse			
Fish			
	Tyler	Rebecca	Sam

Tyler wrote a report on a ______________________.

Rebecca wrote a report on a ______________________.

Sam wrote a report on a ______________________.

In the Sea

What helps a whale float and swim to the surface of the water?

While children may brainstorm many answers based on the reading selection, this hands-on activity demonstrates how blubber helps whales float and rise to the surface to breathe.

Teacher Background Information

Whales are mammals, which means they must come up to the surface to breathe fresh air. That is why their tail fluke moves in an up-and-down position. This helps them to surface and dive. Whales can be very large and heavy animals. Whales, like all mammals, are warm-blooded. That means their body temperature stays the same no matter how cold or warm the water is. The layer of blubber under a whale's skin helps to keep it warm. The blubber also helps whales float and swim closer to the surface.

MATERIALS

(per group)

- ✔ 3–4 small- to medium-sized rocks
- ✔ resealable plastic bag
- ✔ plastic container ($^2/_3$ full of water)
- ✔ spoon
- ✔ vegetable shortening

Procedure

1. Divide the class into groups of four to five children, and give each group a set of materials.
2. Ask a child in each group to place the rocks inside the resealable plastic bag, squeeze most of the air out of the bag, and seal it. (Explain that the bag of rocks represents a whale's heavy body.)
3. Invite a different child to place the "whale" (bag) in the water, and ask all the children to watch what happens.
4. Have another child open the bag, add one to two spoonfuls of "blubber" (shortening), and seal the bag.
5. Ask another child to place the bag in the water again. Tell children to watch to see if the bag will float this time.
6. Encourage children to keep adding blubber (shortening) to the bag until their whale reaches the surface of the water.

Name ______________________ Date ______________

In the Sea

What helps a whale float and swim to the surface of the water?

Results and Conclusions

1. What happened to your "whale" (bag) the first time you put it in the water?

   ____

   Why do you think this happened?

   ____

2. What happened after you added one to two spoonfuls of "blubber" (shortening) to your bag?

   ____

3. How many spoonfuls of blubber did you add in all? ________

4. What helps a whale float and swim to the surface of the water?

   ____

   Why?

   ____

Catch a Clue

What will we learn about in our reading today?

fish

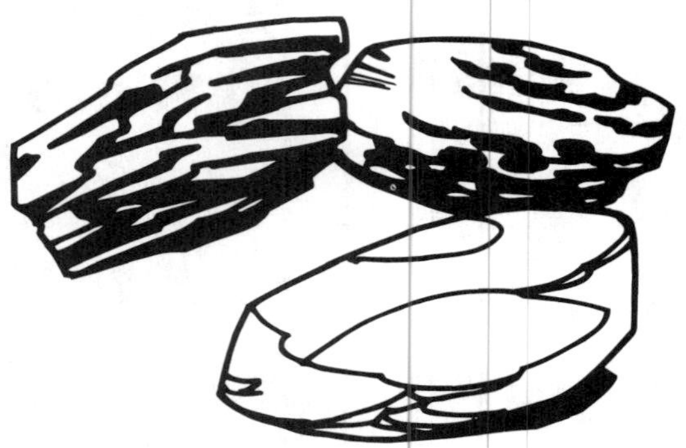

rocks

farm

space

Our Clues

1. **It involves living things.**
2. **The living things give us things we need.**
3. **It is where we get our eggs and milk.**

Concept Map

Facts we already know about **the farm,** and the new facts we have learned

Word Warm-Up

Which words might you expect to find in a story about **the farm?**

zebra	mess	visiting
henhouse	rooster	ice cream
farmer	dairy	raise
blankets	milk	clothes

On the Farm

People who work on farms help us. They grow crops for our food. They also raise animals. We get food from farm animals. We also get wool to make our clothes.

Mrs. Lee's class went to the farm. They wanted to learn about the animals. They saw cows, sheep, and chickens. They saw a dairy cow. The dairy cow gives us milk. This milk is called raw milk. We use this milk to make butter, cheese, and ice cream. The class saw the farmer milk the dairy cow. The raw milk did not look like the milk from the store. It looked light yellow and thick. The farmer said the raw milk goes to the dairy after it comes out of the cow. The people at the dairy take out some of the cream. Each child in the class milked the cow!

The next animals they saw were the sheep. They learned about the sheep's wool. It keeps them warm in the winter. But the sheep get hot in the summer. So the farmer cuts the wool off of the sheep. It is used to make some clothes. The class felt the wool. It was soft. The children had fun touching the wool!

The last stop was the henhouse. Hens lay eggs every day. The class saw the farmer pick up eggs. The farmer sends the eggs to the store for people to buy. Each child held a hen or a rooster. Then, the farmer picked up a hen. It laid an egg right in her hand! The class laughed!

The class said "thank you" to the farmer. They said "good-bye" to the animals. They had a great time learning about the animals. They loved visiting the farm!

Comprehension Questions

Literal Questions

1. Who went on the field trip?
2. What did they see?
3. When did they go to the henhouse?
4. In what order did they see the animals?

Inferential Questions

1. Which animal do you think was the most popular? Why?
2. Did the class have fun? How do you know?
3. What other animals might you see on a farm?
4. What was the biggest surprise on their field trip?

Making Connections

1. If you went to the same farm, what animal would you want to see first? Why?
2. Which of the things the class saw do you think sounds the most interesting? Why?
3. What did the class miss out on that you would want to do on a field trip to the farm? Why?

Name ______________________ Date ____________

Sharpen Your Skills

1. If you put these words in alphabetical order, which word would come before the word "farmer"?

   ❍ sheep ❍ cows
   ❍ hens ❍ roosters

2. How many vowels are in the word "rooster"?

   ❍ 5 ❍ 7
   ❍ 3 ❍ 2

3. In what order did the class see the animals?

   ❍ cows, roosters, sheep ❍ cows, sheep, roosters
   ❍ sheep, roosters, cows ❍ roosters, sheep, cows

4. Which word has the most syllables?

   ❍ cow ❍ horse
   ❍ sheep ❍ rooster

5. Which word finishes the rhyme?

   I want to, but I don't know how.
   Please show me how to milk a ____________.

   ❍ hen ❍ sheep
   ❍ rooster ❍ cow

Name ______________________________ Date ______________

Get Logical

Carlos, Jan, and Trenton were in Mrs. Lee's class. Each child had a favorite animal from the farm. Use the clues below to decide which animal at the farm was each child's favorite.

Clues

1. Trenton's animal was soft and wooly.
2. Jan squirted her friends with this animal!
3. Carlos's animal flew out of his hands.

Cow			
Sheep			
Rooster			
	Carlos	Jan	Trenton

Carlos liked the ______________________ the best.

Jan liked the ______________________ the best.

Trenton liked the ______________________ the best.

On the Farm

How is raw milk different from grocery store milk?

While children may brainstorm many answers based on the reading selection, this hands-on activity demonstrates the process of homogenization.

Teacher Background Information

Raw milk is about one-third butterfat. At the dairy, extra fat is removed from the milk, leaving 4%, 2%, 1%, or no fat (for nonfat milk). The butterfat and milk are used to make butter, cheese, yogurt, sour cream, ice cream, and other dairy products. After the milk and butterfat are separated, two important processes help to make the milk safe and ready for delivery to the grocery store. The dairy pasteurizes the milk by heating it and cooling it quickly. This process kills disease-causing germs. Then, the milk is homogenized. This process evenly distributes the remaining butterfat throughout the milk so that it does not rise to the top (like it does in raw milk). You will need a parent helper for each group of students.

MATERIALS

(per group)

- ✔ 1/2 cup (125 ml) milk (4% or 2%)
- ✔ small empty baby food jar with lid
- ✔ 1/2 cup (125 ml) vegetable oil

Procedure

1. Divide the class into groups of four to five children, assign a parent helper to each group, and give each group a set of materials.
2. Have the parent helper in each group pour milk into the baby food jar until it is one-third full.
3. Ask the parent helper to slowly pour vegetable oil in the jar until there is a yellow layer on top of the milk. (There should be about twice as much milk as oil.)
4. Point out how the oil rises to the top of the milk. (This is what cream or butterfat does naturally in raw milk. The layers separate.)
5. Encourage children to observe the differences in the color and the depth of the two layers of the "raw" milk.
6. Have a child put the lid on the jar of milk.
7. Encourage each group member to take a turn vigorously shaking the jar up and down 20 times.
8. Ask children to place the jar on the table and observe what the contents in the jar look like.

Name ______________________ Date __________

On the Farm

How is raw milk different from grocery store milk?

Results and Conclusions

❶ Color the jar to show what your raw milk looks like, and draw a line from the label words on the right to that part of your raw milk.

Butterfat

Milk

❷ Color the jar to show what your milk looked like after it was shaken. This is your "homogenized" milk.

❸ How is homogenized milk different from raw milk?

____

____

Catch a Clue

What will we learn about in our reading today?

plants

museum

zoo

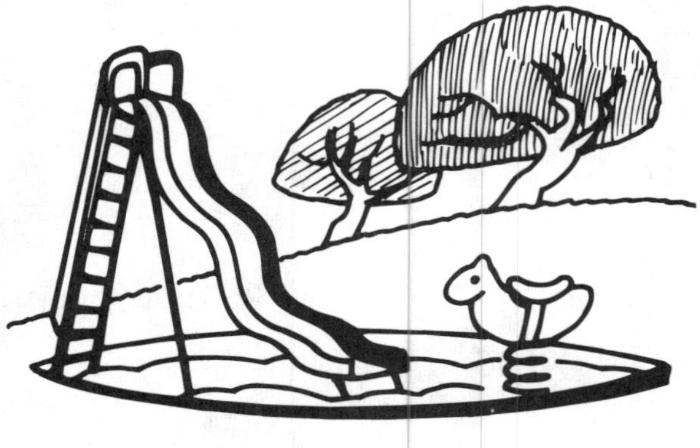

park

Our Clues

1. **It is a place.**
2. **Live animals are there.**
3. **You might see an elephant there.**

Concept Map

Facts we already know about **the zoo,** and the new facts we have learned

Word Warm-Up

Which words might you expect to find in a story about **the zoo?**

predators	farmer	grasslands
home	toucans	cows
endangered	habitat	wild
marsh	roses	porcupines

The Zoo

A zoo is where you can see animals up close. You can also learn about them. You can learn about where they live. Most of the animals at the zoo are wild. Some of them are endangered. This means there are not many of them left in the world.

Sometimes animals do not live long in the wild. They are hunted and killed. At the zoo, they are safe. A good zoo has a large and safe home for each kind of animal. Animals are fed at the zoo. Their homes are cleaned. They are well cared for at the zoo.

How do zoos make homes for the animals? The zoo tries to make it look like their home in the wild. Lions, giraffes, and zebras live in the grasslands. It is warm and dry there. Elephants, monkeys, and toucans live in the jungle. It is hot and wet there. Bears and porcupines live in the forest. It is damp and cool there.

Alligators live in a freshwater marsh. Grass and reeds grow out of the water in a marsh.

What if there were not any zoos? Then, you would not see the animals up close. You could only read about them or see them on TV. Have you gone to a zoo? If you go, look at the animals and their homes. You can think about these things: Do you think the animals are happy? Do you think their homes are clean and safe? You can learn a lot more about animals at a zoo.

Comprehension Questions

Literal Questions

1. What is a zoo?
2. What are some animals that live in a zoo?
3. Why are zoos important?
4. What do animals' homes look like in zoos?

Inferential Questions

1. What other animals do you think would be in a zoo? Why?
2. Why do you think zoos try to make homes for animals that look like their natural homes in the wild?
3. Do you think a toucan would be happy living where an alligator lives? Why or why not?
4. Do you think it is safe to touch the animals at the zoo? Why or why not?

Making Connections

1. If you went to the zoo, what animal would you most like to see? Why?
2. How are zoos different from farms?
3. How are zoos the same as farms?

Name ______________________________ Date ______________

Sharpen Your Skills

❶ If you put these words in alphabetical order, which word would come before the word "hippo"?

❍ porcupine ❍ lion
❍ giraffe ❍ zebra

❷ Which animal lives in a freshwater marsh?

❍ toucan ❍ alligator
❍ zebra ❍ bear

❸ What is the most important reason for having zoos?

❍ so people can look at the animals
❍ to learn about animals and to protect animals
❍ to charge money for visitors
❍ to have a place for school field trips

❹ Which word best fits in this sentence?

A zoo is a place where animals are ____________.

❍ protect ❍ protects
❍ protected ❍ protecting

❺ Which word would finish this analogy?

Cow is to **farm** like ____________ is to **jungle**.

❍ elephant ❍ bear
❍ lion ❍ giraffe

Name ______________________________ Date ______________

Get Logical

There are many animals at the Zany Zoo. The monkeys, giraffes, and elephants have different zookeepers who take care of them. Use the clues below to decide which zookeeper takes care of each group of animals.

Clues

1. Some of Arthur's animals have long front teeth called tusks.
2. Linda needs to stand on a tall ladder to check her animals' teeth.
3. James takes care of animals that swing from tree branches.

Monkeys			
Giraffes			
Elephants			
	Linda	Arthur	James

Linda takes care of the ______________________.

Arthur takes care of the ______________________.

James takes care of the ______________________.

The Zoo

How would you take care of a giraffe, an alligator, or a monkey if you were the zookeeper?

While children may brainstorm many answers based on the reading selection, this hands-on activity demonstrates how environments can be created to meet the needs of various animals.

Teacher Background Information

Zoos are designed to educate people about the great diversity of animal life on earth and to help the public understand the need to conserve and preserve animal habitats. The two most common methods of building zoo environments are using a pit or moat to surround the area (which keeps the animals confined but gives a better view to the public) and using enclosures. An area can be partitioned using a fence or block wall.

MATERIALS

(per pair)

- ✔ shoe box
- ✔ glue
- ✔ clay
- ✔ assorted craft supplies (e.g., pipe cleaners, dried flowers, construction paper, small twigs, grass)
- ✔ toothpicks or craft sticks
- ✔ animal patterns from The Zoo Results and Conclusions reproducible (page 39)
- ✔ scissors
- ✔ crayons or markers
- ✔ tape

Procedure

1. Discuss with the class attributes of a variety of habitats (e.g., grasslands, jungle, freshwater marsh).
2. Discuss and list on the chalkboard the attributes for each animal's (i.e., giraffe, alligator, or monkey) living environment.
3. Have each child find a partner. Ask each pair to pick one of the three animals.
4. Give each pair a set of materials.
5. Invite children to plan how they will create a safe zoo habitat for their animal. (Remind children that their animal must not be able to escape from the zoo.)
6. Have children stand the shoe box on its side horizontally. Have them glue the clay inside the bottom of their shoe box and then build the zoo habitat inside with the craft supplies.
7. Invite children to put toothpicks or craft sticks at the front end of their shoe box to create an enclosure.
8. Encourage children to cut out and color the pattern for their animal, tape a toothpick on the back of their animal cutout, and insert the toothpick into the clay to place their animal in its habitat.

Name ______________________________ Date ______________

The Zoo

How would you take care of a giraffe, an alligator, or a monkey if you were the zookeeper?

Results and Conclusions

1. Which animal did you choose?

____

2. What did you put in its habitat?

____

3. Do you think it is easy or hard to be a zookeeper? ____________ Why?

____

4. How would you take care of a giraffe, an alligator, or a monkey if you were the zookeeper?

____

Cut

Catch a Clue

What will we learn about in our reading today?

life cycles

electricity

day and night

mammals

Our Clues

1. **It involves things that change.**
2. **It involves living things.**
3. **It involves how things grow.**

Concept Map

Facts we already know about **life cycles**, and the new facts we have learned

Word Warm-Up

Which words might you expect to find in a story about **life cycles?**

light	circle	gills
froglet	piglet	sprout
plane	hatches	living
matures	grass	begin

Life Cycles

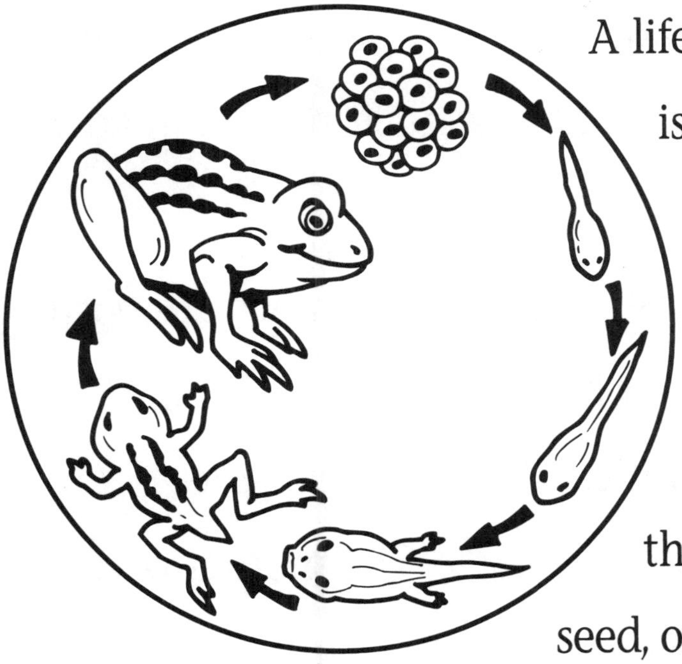

A life cycle keeps repeating itself. It is like a circle story. It is sometimes called the "circle of life." A life cycle begins with an egg, a seed, or a baby. The egg hatches. The seed sprouts. Or, the baby is born. Then, the egg, seed, or baby grows up. Finally, it helps create a new egg, seed, or baby so the circle of life can go on. Each living thing has a life cycle.

The life cycle of a frog begins with an egg. The egg hatches into a tadpole. The tadpole lives in the water. It breathes with gills and has a tail. The tadpole forms lungs and legs as it grows. When this happens, the gills and tail go away. It is now a froglet. The froglet loses its tail and grows into a frog. Now that it is a frog, it lives mostly on land. Then, the frog lays eggs to repeat the life cycle.

The life cycle of many plants begins with a seed. The

seed becomes a sprout. The sprout grows into a plant. The plant matures. Then, it drops more seeds. Those seeds can be planted to begin the life cycle again.

The life cycle of a rabbit begins when baby bunnies are born. The mother rabbit makes a "form." This is a hole dug in the ground to hide herself and her bunnies. It keeps them safe. Bunnies do not have hair when they are born. The mother covers them with fur and soft plants to keep them warm and dry. The bunnies grow fur in one week. Their eyes and ears also open. The bunnies take their first hops in two weeks. Then, two days later, they leave to take care of themselves. They grow to become rabbits. Then, some will have more baby bunnies to repeat their life cycle.

Every living thing has a life cycle. Look all around you. What is the life cycle of each living thing that you see?

Comprehension Questions

Literal Questions

1. What is a life cycle?
2. What is the life cycle of a frog?
3. What do plants begin as?
4. What is another name for a life cycle?

Inferential Questions

1. What do you think would happen if an animal could not continue its life cycle?
2. Why do we need to learn about life cycles?
3. Why do you think a frog's life cycle has more stages than a rabbit's life cycle?
4. What do you think the life cycle of a chicken is?

Making Connections

1. Is your life cycle more like the life cycle of a plant, frog, or rabbit? Why?
2. What do people do that can hurt the life cycle of some animals?
3. What other things does the "circle of life" remind you of?

Name ______________________________ Date ______________

Sharpen Your Skills

1. If you put the life cycle stages of a frog in alphabetical order, which stage would come first?
   - ❍ frog
   - ❍ froglet
   - ❍ egg
   - ❍ tadpole

2. Which animal's life cycle begins with an egg?
   - ❍ rabbit
   - ❍ plant
   - ❍ flower
   - ❍ frog

3. What is the describing word (adjective) in this sentence?
   Most frogs hatch from tiny eggs.
   - ❍ tiny
   - ❍ frogs
   - ❍ eggs
   - ❍ from

4. Which word best fits this sentence?
   Reptiles, amphibians, and ________ hatch from eggs.
   - ❍ hamsters
   - ❍ roses
   - ❍ birds
   - ❍ trees

5. Which word would finish this analogy?
   Tadpole is to **frog** like **seed** is to ____________.
   - ❍ plant
   - ❍ butterfly
   - ❍ bird
   - ❍ rabbit

Name ______________________________ Date ______________

Get Logical

Each second-grade class at Weaver Elementary School decided to learn about the life cycle of a different living thing. Use the clues below to decide which creature each room learned about.

Clues

1. Room 3 learned about a living thing that can fly.
2. Room 2 learned about an animal that looks a lot like its mother when it is born.
3. There were tadpoles in Room 4.

Horse			
Frog			
Ladybug			
	Room 2	Room 3	Room 4

Room 2 learned about a ______________________.

Room 3 learned about a ______________________.

Room 4 learned about a ______________________.

Life Cycles

How can we help the life cycle of a tomato plant continue?

While children may brainstorm many answers based on the reading selection, this hands-on activity demonstrates the growth differences between raw tomato seeds and processed, packaged tomato seeds.

Teacher Background Information

Each plant or animal's life cycle takes a different amount of time. Insect life cycles are usually short, often less than a year. However, most animal life cycles last over a period of many years. Plant life cycles also vary in length. Annuals are plants that complete their life cycle in one year. Biennials are plants that have a two-year life cycle. Perennials are plants with life cycles that last over a period of many years. Seeds from a fresh fruit or vegetable often do not sprout as well as packaged seeds from a plant nursery. Packaged seeds have been dried and treated with chemicals that preserve them and aid in sprouting.

MATERIALS

(per group)

- ✔ Observations Over Time reproducible (page 49)
- ✔ 1 plastic knife
- ✔ 1 tomato
- ✔ potting soil
- ✔ 2 medium-sized flowerpots or plastic containers
- ✔ water
- ✔ 2 labels
- ✔ 1/2 package of tomato seeds

Procedure

1. Divide the class into groups of four to five children, and give each group a set of materials.
2. Have a child in each group use the plastic knife to cut the tomato in half.
3. Invite children to observe the inside of the tomato and discuss what they see.
4. Have another child place potting soil in each flowerpot until it is two-thirds full.
5. Ask another child to place half of the tomato in one of the pots, cover it with more soil, and add water until all of the soil is moist.
6. Select a child to write *Fresh Seeds* on one label and stick it to this pot.
7. Invite children to observe the tomato seeds from the package and discuss what they see.
8. Have a child sprinkle a few seeds over the soil in the second flowerpot, cover it with more soil, and add water until all of the soil is moist.
9. Select another child to write *Dry Seeds* on the second label and stick it to this pot.
10. Invite children to place both pots in a sunny location.
11. Encourage children to water both pots every few days as needed, observe what changes are happening, and record their observations on their Observations Over Time reproducible.

Name ______________________________ Date ______________

Life Cycles

How can we help the life cycle of a tomato plant continue?

Observations Over Time

Date	Fresh Seeds	Dry Seeds

Name ______________________ Date ____________

Life Cycles

How can we help the life cycle of a tomato plant continue?

Results and Conclusions

1. How were the fresh seeds different from the seeds in the package?

   ____

2. Did your fresh tomato seeds sprout? ________

   If so, how many days did it take? ________

3. Did your dry seeds sprout? ________

   If so, how many days did it take? ________

4. Did the "Fresh Seeds" or the "Dry Seeds" pot grow better after 10 days?

   ____

5. What will the tomato plants make if you let the life cycle continue longer?

   ____

6. How can we help the life cycle of a tomato plant continue?

   ____

Catch a Clue

What will we learn about in our reading today?

moth

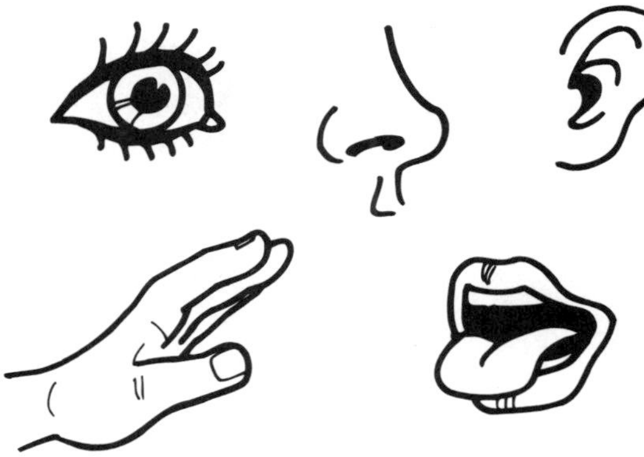

five senses

rocks

sand

Our Clues

1. **They are outside on the ground.**
2. **Some are very big, but most of them are small.**
3. **They are not alive.**

Concept Map

Facts we already know about **rocks**, and the new facts we have learned

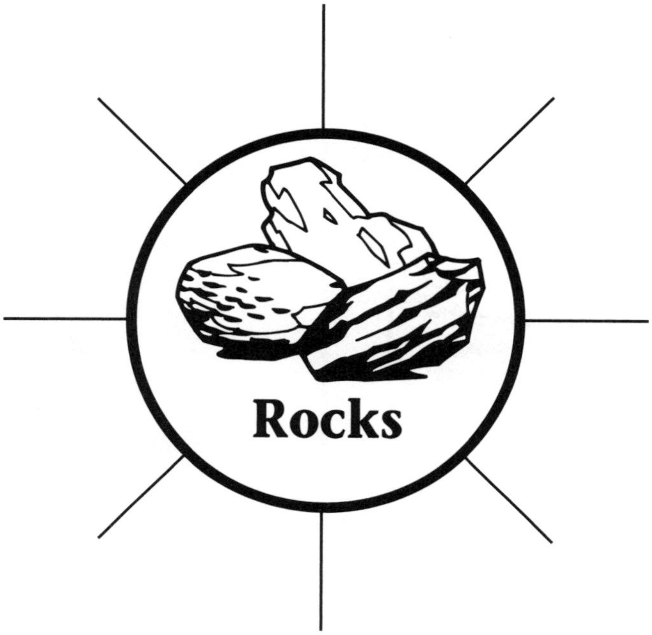

Word Warm-Up

Which words might you expect to find in a story about **rocks?**

crust	hard	scientists
granite	diamond	clouds
graphite	wind	minerals
colors	alphabet	ground

Rocks

What are rocks? You see them all the time. They are in the street. They are at your school. They are in your yard. What are they made of?

Rocks come in many shapes and sizes. Each type of rock is made up of one or more minerals. Minerals are like the letters of the alphabet. Most words are made up of a few letters. In the same way, most rocks are made up of a few minerals. When the minerals have different colors, we can see them in a rock. This may make the rock look speckled or splotched with colors. A speckled rock you might easily find is granite. It looks like small bits of salt and pepper mixed together.

Some of the minerals in a rock have the same colors. If they do, you cannot tell what the rock is made of when you look at it. Scientists have ways to test rocks to see what minerals are in them. Some minerals are hard. Some are soft. Some are shiny. Some are dull. The hardest mineral is a diamond. It can scratch or cut almost anything! Diamonds are used to make jewelry. They are used in machines to cut hard things, too. Talc and graphite are minerals. They are very soft. You can scratch them with your fingernail. Talc is ground up and used for baby and bath powder. Your pencil lead is made of graphite. It is so soft that it rubs off when you write.

Go on a rock hunt. Look closely at the rocks you find. You might see some of the minerals that make up the rock. You may even want to start a rock collection!

Comprehension Questions

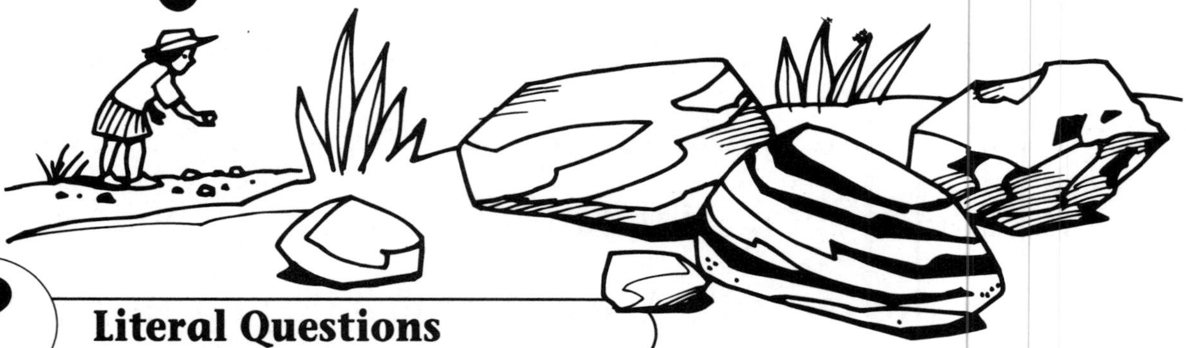

Literal Questions

1. What is a rock made out of?
2. Where can you find rocks?
3. Which is the hardest mineral?
4. What is talc used for?

Inferential Questions

1. Other than your fingernail, what might you use to test how hard or soft a rock is?
2. Where are rocks found other than the earth's surface?
3. What kind of groups would you make when sorting rocks into a collection?
4. Do you think other minerals besides a diamond could be used to make jewelry? Which ones?

Making Connections

1. What is the most common color of rocks you have seen?
2. Have you ever had a rock collection? Would you want one?
3. Where could you go to find the rocks for a rock collection?

Name ______________________ Date ____________

Sharpen Your Skills

1. If you put these words in alphabetical order, which word would come before the word "diamond"?

   ❍ rocks ❍ crust
   ❍ granite ❍ mantle

2. Rocks are **composed of** different kinds of minerals.
   What do the words "composed of" mean?

   ❍ tired of ❍ made out of
   ❍ full of ❍ missing

3. Talc is a mineral found in rocks.
   Which word is a person, place, or thing (noun) in this sentence?

   ❍ talc ❍ is
   ❍ found ❍ in

4. Which word best fits this sentence?
   Melted minerals cool and harden to __________ rocks.

   ❍ became ❍ become
   ❍ becoming ❍ becomed

5. Which word would finish this analogy?
   Milk is to **ice cream** like __________ are to **rocks.**

   ❍ streams ❍ mountains
   ❍ minerals ❍ ice cubes

Name ______________________ Date ____________

Get Logical

Sarah, Laura, and Maria each had a rock collection. Each girl collected only one kind of rock. Use the clues below to decide which type of rock each girl collected.

Clues

1. Laura collected rocks that had been in streams and rivers for a long time.
2. Sarah wore gloves when she picked up her favorite rocks.
3. Maria collected rocks that had different mineral colors.

Speckled Rocks			
Smooth Rocks			
Sharp Rocks			
	Sarah	Laura	Maria

Sarah collected ______________________.

Laura collected ______________________.

Maria collected ______________________.

Rocks

What kinds of rocks can you find on a rock hunt?

While children may brainstorm many answers based on the reading selection, this hands-on activity demonstrates how to classify rocks by hardness using the "scratch test."

Teacher Background Information

Some minerals exist in their pure form in the earth's crust. However, most minerals have combined to make rocks. There are three types of rocks—sedimentary, igneous, and metamorphic. Sedimentary rocks, or layered rocks, are made from layers of sediment that pile up at the bottom of oceans and lakes. Gradually, the particles (e.g., clay, sand, pebbles, crumbled seashells) are cemented together and harden into rock. Sandstone, limestone, and shale are examples of sedimentary rocks. Most sedimentary rocks are softer and can be scratched with a nail. Igneous rocks, or fire-formed rocks, are created from magma or lava. The magma may get pushed up into the crust, where it can remain trapped. This magma cools off very slowly. As it cools, mineral crystals form. The slower it cools, the larger the crystals that are formed. Speckled rocks like granite are formed from trapped magma. If the magma reaches the earth's surface, it is called lava. The third type of rock is called metamorphic rock. This is a changed rock. It used to be an igneous or a sedimentary rock. Due to tremendous heat and pressure within the earth's crust, these rocks were changed into metamorphic rock. Slate and marble are examples of metamorphic rocks. Metamorphic rocks are generally harder rocks, too.

MATERIALS

(per child)

- ✔ Rock Hunt Collection Data reproducible (page 60)
- ✔ small plastic bag
- ✔ 4 rocks from class rock hunt
- ✔ nail

Procedure

1. Give each child a small plastic bag.
2. Take your class outside for a rock hunt. Ask children to look for four different rocks and put them in their bag.
3. Give each child a Rock Hunt Collection Data reproducible. Ask children to lay each rock in a separate box on the left-hand side of their paper.
4. Invite children to try to scratch each rock with their fingernail. (If they can, it is a "soft" rock.)
5. Give each child a nail. (Remind children to be very careful using the nail and to only use it to test the rock.) Ask children to try to scratch each rock with the nail. (If they can, it is a "medium hard" rock. If they cannot, it is a "very hard" rock.)
6. Encourage children to classify their rocks using their reproducible. Ask them to check off the characteristics of each rock.

Name ______________________________ Date ______________

Rocks

What kinds of rocks can you find on a rock hunt?

Rock Hunt Collection Data

Rock	Soft	Medium Hard	Very Hard	Smooth	Rough	Light	Dark	Small	Large

Name ______________________ Date ____________

Rocks

What kinds of rocks can you find on a rock hunt?

Results and Conclusions

1. How many rocks could you scratch with your fingernail? ________

2. How many rocks could you scratch with a nail? ________

3. How many rocks could you not scratch at all? ________

4. Which rock is your favorite? ______________ Why?

   ____

5. What kinds of rocks did you find on your rock hunt?

   ____

   ____

   ____

Catch a Clue

What will we learn about in our reading today?

Sun

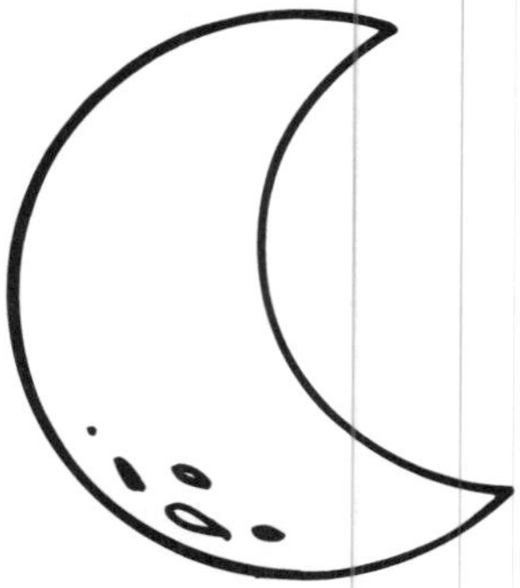

Moon

Neptune

Earth

1. **You can see it from Earth.**
2. **It has light.**
3. **It is extremely hot.**

Concept Map

Facts we already know about **the Sun,** and the new facts we have learned

Word Warm-Up

Which words might you expect to find in a story about **the Sun?**

Moon	turns	Earth
seasons	rocket	plants
day	star	bricks
million	tilts	rotates

The Sun

Did you know that the Sun is a star? The Sun is much closer to the Earth than other stars are. That is why it looks so much bigger than the other stars in the sky. Even though the Sun is our closest star, it is far away. The Sun is much bigger than the Earth. The Sun is so big that you could fit over one million Earths inside of it!

Where does the Sun go at night? It does not come up in the morning and go down at night. The Earth turns around and around. We say it rotates. It is day when our part of the Earth is facing the Sun. It is night when our part of the Earth is facing away from the Sun. One day on Earth is 24 hours long. This is how long it takes the Earth to turn all the way around one time. As our Earth turns, it also moves around the Sun. It takes one year for the Earth to go all the way around the Sun.

The Earth tilts to one side when it spins around. Can you do that? Can you stand up and lean over to one side? Can you turn around at the same time? The Earth can. The way the Earth tilts is important because it gives us our seasons. They are winter, spring, summer, and fall. Our part of the Earth tilts toward the Sun in the summer. We get more sunlight in the summer. This makes it hotter in the summer. In the winter, our part of the Earth tilts away from the Sun. We get less sunlight so it feels colder. It takes one year for all of the seasons to pass.

We could not live without the Sun. It gives us heat and light. There would not be any plants, animals, or people on the Earth if we did not have the Sun. The Sun makes things grow. Everything on Earth needs the Sun.

Comprehension Questions

Literal Questions

1. What is the Sun?
2. Who or what needs the Sun? Why?
3. What does the Sun give us?
4. How does the Earth move in relation to the Sun?

Inferential Questions

1. What would happen to us if there were no Sun?
2. What do you think would happen to something that stayed outside on a sunny day too long? Why?
3. Do you think it is a good idea to look directly at the Sun? Why or why not?
4. Could we ever travel to the Sun? Why or why not?

Making Connections

1. What do you like to do on a sunny day?
2. What is your favorite season? Why?
3. Why should you use sunscreen when you go outside on a sunny day?

Name ______________________________ Date ______________

Sharpen Your Skills

❶ If you put these words in alphabetical order, which word would come after the word "star"?

❍ heat ❍ Moon
❍ Earth ❍ tilt

❷ The Earth **rotates** to give us day and night.

What does the word "rotates" mean?

❍ spins ❍ travels
❍ shines ❍ flips over

❸ What is the describing word (adjective) in this sentence?

The Sun is a bright star in the sky.

❍ Sun ❍ bright
❍ star ❍ sky

❹ Which word in the following sentence is made of two smaller words (compound word)?

When the Sun is facing our part of the Earth, we have daytime.

❍ facing ❍ daytime
❍ when ❍ Earth

❺ Which word would finish this analogy?

Sun is to __________ like **rose** is to **flower.**

❍ star ❍ planet
❍ shiny ❍ Moon

Name ______________________________ Date ______________

Get Logical

Seasons are created when the Earth goes around the Sun. Orly, Mackenzie, and Pedro each have a different favorite season. Use the clues below to decide which season is each person's favorite.

Clues

1. Mackenzie loves to ski and snowboard.
2. Pedro likes to swim.
3. Orly likes to watch the baby birds hatch in their nests.

Winter			
Summer			
Spring			
	Orly	Mackenzie	Pedro

Orly's favorite season is ______________________.

Mackenzie's favorite season is ______________________.

Pedro's favorite season is ______________________.

The Sun

What kinds of living things need the Sun to help them grow?

While children may brainstorm many answers based on the reading selection, this hands-on activity demonstrates how a plant will grow towards the sunlight it is given and how plants grow more in summer than in winter because they receive more direct sunlight.

Teacher Background Information

Without the Sun, green plants would die because they need light from the Sun to make their food. Because all living things feed on plants or animals that have eaten plants, without green plants, all life on Earth would die. Plants grow toward the light to get as much light as possible. Plants will grow straight up if light is all around them. They will grow toward one side if light is only coming from that side. Due to the tilt of the Earth, sunlight strikes our part of the Earth at an angle during the winter. Plants receive less sunlight at this time. During the summer, we receive more direct rays. This makes us feel warmer and also helps plants to grow more. Prepare one shoe box per group before the class begins this experiment. Cut a 2" (5 cm) square out of the top on one end of each box lid. Use black spray paint to completely paint each shoe box on the inside and out. Keep one cup with planted seeds on the windowsill as a control plant to show children the difference when it is not put in a black box.

MATERIALS

(per group)

- ✔ Observation Log reproducible (page 71)
- ✔ small clear plastic cup
- ✔ soil
- ✔ 5 lima beans
- ✔ water
- ✔ painted shoe box

Procedure

1. Divide the class into groups of four to five children, and give each group a set of materials.
2. Invite a child to fill the plastic cup halfway with soil. Ask him or her to place the lima beans in the cup with soil.
3. Have another child cover the lima beans with more soil and water the soil until it is moist.
4. Ask another child to put the cup in the shoe box at the end opposite of the hole.
5. Invite a different child to put their box on a counter near sunlight.
6. Have children check their shoe boxes every other day (approximately five times over ten days). Ask them to record their observations on their Observation Log reproducible.

Name ______________________________ Date ______________

The Sun

What kinds of living things need the Sun to help them grow?

Observation Log

Date	What is happening?

Name ______________________ Date ____________

The Sun

What kinds of living things need the Sun to help them grow?

Results and Conclusions

1. Did the lima beans grow? ________

   How did they grow?

   ____

2. Do you think the plant would grow if there were not a hole in the box? ________

   Why or why not?

   ____

   ____

3. What kinds of living things need the Sun to help them grow?

   ____

   ____

Catch a Clue

What will we learn about in our reading today?

planets

storms

the sun

clouds

Our Clues

1. **They are in the sky.**
2. **They are made of water droplets and ice crystals.**
3. **They tell us about the weather.**

Concept Map

Facts we already know about **clouds,** and the new facts we have learned

Word Warm-Up

Which words might you expect to find in a story about **clouds?**

feathers	droplets	basic
water	tables	condense
clock	vapor	cumulus
layers	thunder	float

Clouds

What are clouds made of? Clouds are made of lots of small water droplets or ice crystals. Clouds start to form when the sun warms the water in the oceans, rivers, and lakes. Some of the water turns into water vapor. It goes up into the sky. The water vapor turns into small water droplets. These make clouds. The droplets float in the air because they are so small. The droplets can stick to each other. When they do, they get bigger. It rains when they are big and heavy.

There are three basic types of clouds. One type of cloud is a stratus cloud. Stratus clouds form low in the sky and close to the ground. They look like flat gray layers. The layers look like a gray blanket that covers the sky. Stratus clouds can block the sun. If you see these clouds, there is a chance of light rain.

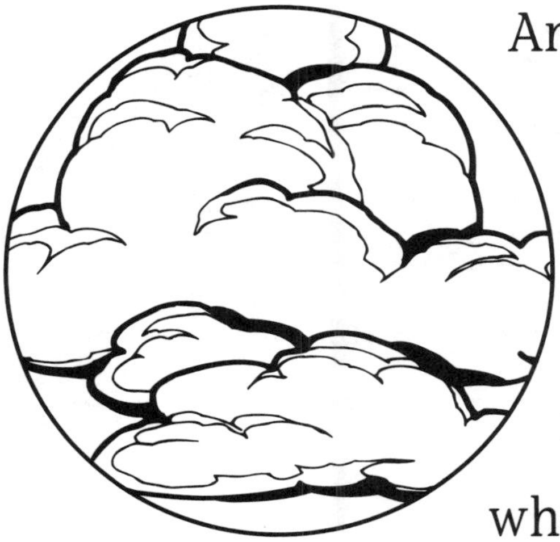

Another type of cloud is a cumulus cloud. Cumulus clouds look white and fluffy like cotton balls. They are flat on the bottom and puffy on the top. They form in the middle of the sky. It will be a nice day when you see these fluffy clouds.

The third type of cloud is a cirrus cloud. Cirrus clouds look like feathers or curled hair. They form high up in the sky and always have small ice crystals in them. If you see them, the weather is calm for now but can change soon.

Sometimes cumulus clouds get a lot more water droplets. Then, they grow bigger and taller. They change into huge, dark clouds called cumulonimbus clouds. These are storm clouds. They bring us a lot of rain, lightning, and thunder. Look in the sky. Do you see some clouds? What types of clouds do you see? Can you tell what the weather will be like?

Comprehension Questions

Literal Questions

1. What are clouds made of?
2. How are clouds formed?
3. What are the four different types of clouds?
4. What does each type of cloud look like?

Inferential Questions

1. If you wanted to watch the rain, what clouds would you hope to see in the sky?
2. Which type of cloud can sometimes look like an animal shape?
3. Why are there some days without any clouds?
4. If we flew through the clouds in an airplane, what would we see?

Making Connections

1. Which type of cloud can you see in the sky right now?
2. Which type of cloud is the most interesting to you?
3. What shapes can you see in the clouds?

Name ______________________________ Date ______________

Sharpen Your Skills

1 If you put these words in alphabetical order, which word would come first?

❍ stratus ❍ droplets
❍ vapor ❍ clouds

2 Stratus clouds can look like **layers** in the sky.

What does the word "layers" mean?

❍ stacks ❍ feathers
❍ patterns ❍ cotton balls

3 What is the action word (verb) in this sentence?

We are learning about different kinds of clouds.

❍ about ❍ clouds
❍ different ❍ learning

4 Which word best fits this sentence?

Stratus clouds ________ out across the sky like a blanket.

❍ slip ❍ line
❍ spread ❍ flip

5 Which word would finish this analogy?

Cirrus is to **feathery** like **cumulus** is to ______________.

❍ fluffy ❍ invisible
❍ flat ❍ stratus

Name ______________________________ Date ______________

Get Logical

Mr. Aguilar's class was learning about clouds every day. They checked the types of clouds in the sky. Use the clues below to decide which type of cloud they saw on each day.

Clues

1. The stratus clouds were in the sky at the end of the week.
2. The fluffy clouds were in the sky before Wednesday.
3. The feathery clouds were in the sky before the stratus clouds.

Cumulus			
Stratus			
Cirrus			
	Monday	Wednesday	Friday

On Monday they saw ______________________ clouds.

On Wednesday they saw ______________________ clouds.

On Friday they saw ______________________ clouds.

Clouds

How can you tell one type of cloud from another?

While children may brainstorm many answers based on the reading selection, this hands-on activity will help them create a reference booklet to use when they view and classify clouds.

Teacher Background Information

The three main types of clouds are stratus, cumulus, and cirrus. Many variations of these clouds exist. The cumulonimbus storm cloud is the easiest for young children to recognize.

Prepare a blank book for each child before the class begins this project. Fold two 9" x 12" (23 cm x 30.5 cm) pieces of blue construction paper in half. Then, place one 6" x 9" (15 cm x 23 cm) piece of blue construction paper between the folded pages to create a book, and staple it along the folded edge.

MATERIALS

(per child)

- ✔ Cloud Cutouts reproducible (page 82)
- ✔ premade blank book
- ✔ scissors
- ✔ glue
- ✔ 11 cotton balls
- ✔ talcum powder mixed with powdered black tempera paint
- ✔ black pen
- ✔ 2" x 4" (5 cm x 10 cm) yellow construction paper

Procedure

1. Have children cut out the "Clouds" title from their reproducible, glue it to the front of their book, and write their name below the title. Tell children to cut out the four cloud information boxes.
2. Invite children to create each type of cloud as follows:
   - Cirrus Clouds—Ask children to scatter small dots of glue over the top half of the first page in their book. Have them tear a cotton ball into small, thin pieces. Tell them to place the pieces on the glue dots. Invite them to glue their "Cirrus Clouds" box at the bottom of this page.
   - Cumulus Clouds—Draw a cumulus cloud on the chalkboard. Ask children to use a pencil to copy your drawing on the next page. Have them tear two cotton balls into many small pieces. Invite them to spread glue over their cloud shape and place the cotton pieces on the glue to fill in the shape. Have them glue their "Cumulus Clouds" box at the bottom of this page.
   - Stratus Clouds—Invite children to stretch two cotton balls into a long "hot dog" shape. Ask them to glue one piece on the center of the next page and glue the other piece above it but to the right. Have them glue their "Stratus Clouds" box at the bottom of this page.
   - Cumulonimbus Clouds—Draw a cumulonimbus cloud on the chalkboard. Ask children to use a pencil to copy your drawing on the next page. Have children tear six cotton balls into many pieces. Invite them to spread glue over their cloud shape and place the cotton pieces on it. Give each child a small amount of gray talcum powder. Ask children to use their finger to dab bits of talcum powder over the bottom of the cloud until it looks gray. Have them use a black pen to draw raindrops coming from the cloud. Have each child cut a lightning bolt from a piece of yellow construction paper. Invite children to glue their lightning bolt coming out of the bottom of the cloud. Ask children to glue their "Cumulonimbus Clouds" box at the bottom of this page. Encourage children to go outside and use their cloud book to help them identify the clouds they see.

Clouds

How can you tell one type of cloud from another?

Cloud Cutouts

Cirrus Clouds These thin and feathery clouds are high in the sky. They are a sign of calm weather now, but it can change soon.	**Stratus Clouds** These flat clouds are low in the sky. They show a chance of light rain.
Cumulus Clouds These puffy clouds are in the middle of the sky. They signal a nice day.	**Cumulonimbus Clouds** These dark, tall, and huge clouds bring thunderstorms.

Name ______________________ Date __________

Clouds

How can you tell one type of cloud from another?

Results and Conclusions

1. What type of clouds do you see outside today?

____

2. Did you see more than one type of cloud? ________ If so, what types were they?

____

3. What do you think the weather will be like today?

____

4. How can you tell one type of cloud from another?

____

____

Catch a Clue

What will we learn about in our reading today?

earthworms

bees

storms

clouds

Our Clues

1. **They are in the sky.**
2. **They can be dangerous.**
3. **They are part of our weather system.**

Concept Map

Facts we already know about **stormy weather,** and the new facts we have learned

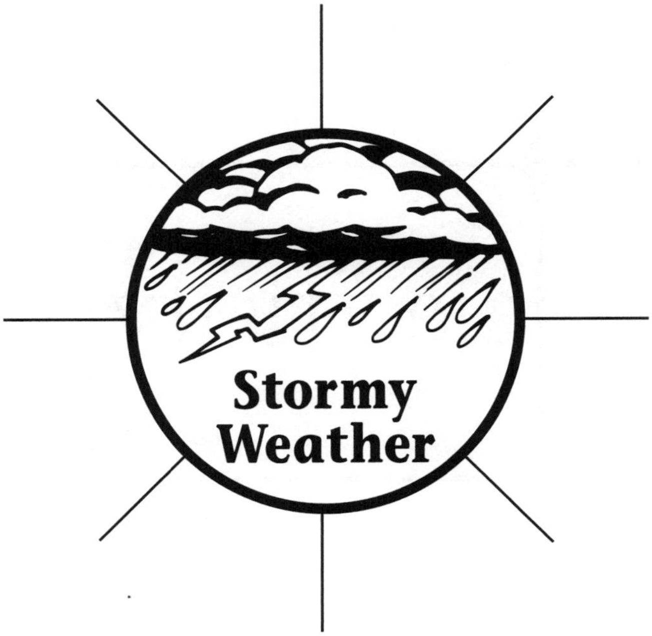

Word Warm-Up

Which words might you expect to find in a story about **stormy weather?**

tiger	lightning	thunder
safe	electricity	water
condense	wind	dangerous
pellet	ice crystal	droplets

Stormy Weather

Have you ever gotten soaked in a rainstorm? Have you seen a flash of lightning? Have you heard the boom of thunder in a thunderstorm? What do you think makes these stormy sights and sounds?

The air around the earth acts like a sponge. The air can soak up a lot of water. It is called water vapor. We cannot see it. Warm air takes water vapor up into the sky. The water vapor begins to cool off and forms a cloud. The cloud is full of water droplets. When a cloud cannot hold any more water droplets, the droplets fall to the ground. This is rain.

A thunderstorm begins when warm and damp air rises very fast. This forms cumulus clouds. This warm air bumps into cooler air that is falling down to the ground. Then, more damp air will rise and condense. When this happens, the cumulus clouds start to grow big and tall. They become huge storm clouds called cumulonimbus clouds.

You may hear thunder in a storm. Thunder is the sound that lightning makes when it goes through the air. You see lightning first. Then, you hear thunder. This is because light travels faster than sound.

Thunderstorms have lightning. This happens when the air rises fast and rubs on the water droplets in the storm clouds. These clouds can make a huge spark. The spark can go from one cloud to another cloud. It can go from a cloud to the land. We see the spark as lightning.

Thunderstorms can be scary. Stay inside during a storm. If you are outside, move away from trees and water. Follow these tips to stay safe.

Comprehension Questions

Literal Questions

1. What makes a thunderstorm?
2. What makes lightning?
3. How can you stay safe in a thunderstorm?
4. Why do you see lightning before you hear thunder?

Inferential Questions

1. Why do we need rain?
2. If you are camping in a tent during a thunderstorm, what should you do?
3. Should you swim in a pool during a thunderstorm? Why or why not?
4. How do you think thunderstorms can cause problems for people, plants, and animals?

Making Connections

1. How do you feel when there is a thunderstorm?
2. What safety rules should you follow during a storm?
3. What kinds of storms have you been in before?

Name ______________________________ Date ______________

Sharpen Your Skills

1. If you put these words in alphabetical order, which word would go between the words "rain" and "thunder"?

   ❍ storm ❍ lightning
   ❍ clouds ❍ air

2. You need to follow the safety rules to **protect** yourself.

   What does the word "protect" mean?

   ❍ take care of ❍ tell
   ❍ look at ❍ prove

3. What is the action word (verb) in this sentence?

   Lightning can strike from cloud to cloud or from a cloud to the ground.

   ❍ cloud ❍ lightning
   ❍ ground ❍ strike

4. Which word best fits this sentence?

   Light travels ________ than sound, so we see the lightning before we hear the thunder.

   ❍ fast ❍ faster
   ❍ fastest ❍ fasting

5. Which word would finish this analogy?

   Ringing is to a **telephone** like __________ is to a **storm.**

   ❍ lightning ❍ rain
   ❍ thunder ❍ clouds

Name ______________________________ Date ______________

Get Logical

Alex, Rodney, and Cindi remembered the thunderstorm safety rules over vacation. Use the clues below to decide what each child was doing when the storm hit.

Clues

1. Rodney did not go outside to look at the lightning. He watched from his window.
2. Alex got out of the fishing boat and walked back up to the campground. Then, he went in the camper.
3. Cindi moved away from the tall tree.

Camping at the Lake			
Watching Television			
Hiking in the Forest			
	Alex	Rodney	Cindi

Alex was ______________________________.

Rodney was ______________________________.

Cindi was ______________________________.

Stormy Weather

How could you create sleet or snow crystals without a storm?

While children may brainstorm many answers based on the reading selection, this hands-on activity demonstrates how sleet and ice crystals form.

Teacher Background Information

Rain is the most common form of precipitation. Rain occurs whenever the temperature of the air in a cloud and the air closer to the ground is above freezing. Raindrops coalesce in the clouds and fall to the ground. Snow is the most common form of solid precipitation. Snow crystals are never raindrops first. The water vapor freezes and forms snow right in the clouds. Then, the snowflakes fall to the ground. This occurs when the temperature of the air in the cloud is below freezing. When the air near the ground is warmer, the snowflakes melt together and form large clumps of wet, sticky snow. When the air near the ground is cold, the dry, fluffy snowflakes fall separately. Sleet starts out as raindrops but freezes on the way down to the ground.

MATERIALS

(for one whole-class demonstration)

- ✔ large, tall, empty can (e.g., juice or large coffee can)
- ✔ crushed ice
- ✔ table salt
- ✔ small dish towel
- ✔ piece of waxed paper (larger than the can)
- ✔ water

Procedure

1. Call on children to assist you with each step of the demonstration.
2. Fill the can with a layer of crushed ice.
3. Add a layer of table salt. (Your ice layer should be twice as thick as the salt layer.)
4. Continue to add both layers until you fill the can.
5. Use the dish towel to pack down the layers in the can.
6. Place the piece of waxed paper next to the can, and put a few drops of water in the middle of it. Make one drop a bit larger than the others. (These represent raindrops.)
7. Wrap the towel around the can to lift it, and then place it on top of the "raindrops" on the waxed paper.
8. Remove the towel.
9. Wait several minutes, and have children observe the outside of the can.
10. After you see ice crystals covering most of the sides of the can, use the towel to help remove the can from the waxed paper.
11. Invite children to observe what happened to the raindrops on the waxed paper.

Name ______________________ Date ____________

Stormy Weather

How could you create sleet or snow crystals without a storm?

Results and Conclusions

1. What happened to the sides of the can?

____

2. If these ice crystals fell from the sky, what would you call them?

____

Why do you think they formed?

____

3. What happened to the "raindrops" on the waxed paper?

____

4. What is the difference between the way sleet and snow are formed?

____

5. How did you create sleet or snow crystals without a storm?

____

Catch a Clue

What will we learn about in our reading today?

sound

soil

matter

lightning

Our Clues

1. **It makes up things all around us.**
2. **It comes in different shapes and sizes.**
3. **It can be a solid, liquid, or gas.**

Concept Map

Facts we already know about **matter,** and the new facts we have learned

Word Warm-Up

Which words might you expect to find in a story about **matter?**

solid	light	help
change	balloon	liquid
matter	containers	lemon
measure	gas	steam

Matter

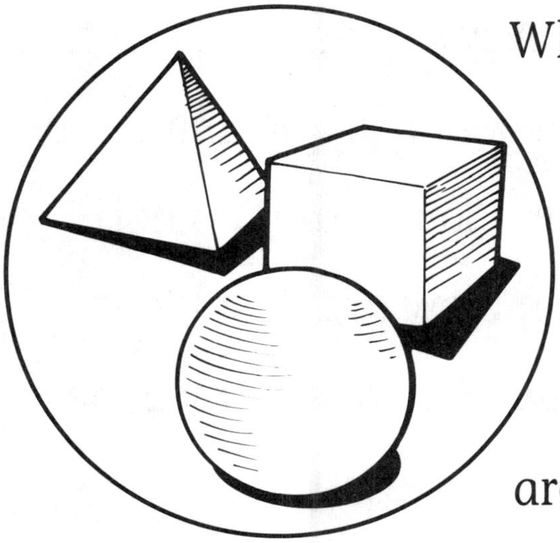

What is matter? Matter is something that takes up space and has weight. Matter is all around you. Even the air you breathe is made of matter! Matter can be a solid, a liquid, or a gas. These are called the three "states" of matter.

Anything that has a size and shape is called a solid. A solid can be hard or soft. Wood, glass, rubber, and metal are all solids. Look all around you. What solids do you see?

A liquid has an exact size. It does not have an exact shape. But, we can measure its size. Your mom does this when she cooks. We can pour a liquid. This lets it change its shape to fit other containers. If you put milk in a tall glass, it would be the shape of that tall glass. If you put it in a short bowl, it would be the shape of the bowl. Milk, oil, and juice are all liquids.

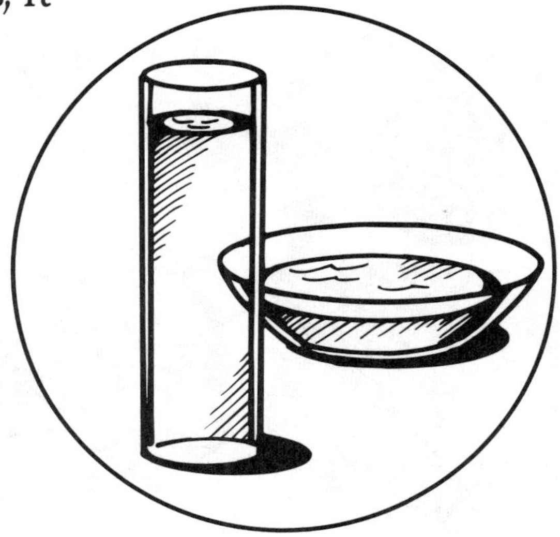

A gas does not have a shape or size. A gas spreads out until it fills what it is in. A gas is special. It can get bigger or smaller to fit in something. Air and oxygen are gases. Some gases do not have color so we cannot see them. You can blow gas. Just blow bubbles through a straw in a glass of water. This lets you see the bubbles of gas.

Matter can change from one state to another by heating or cooling. If you cool water, it will freeze and become ice. Ice is a solid. If the ice melts, it turns back into water (a liquid). If you heat water, it will boil. Then, it turns into steam. Steam is a gas. The steam can cool off. Then, it will turn back into water (a liquid). No matter is lost when this happens. The way it looks is just changed. What other examples of matter can you find?

Comprehension Questions

Literal Questions

1. What is matter?
2. What are the three "states" of matter?
3. Where is matter?
4. What state of matter is water?

Inferential Questions

1. Do you think clay is a solid? Why or why not?
2. What would happen if you left a stick of butter out in the sun?
3. Sally watched her helium-filled balloon float up into the sky. Why do you think this happened?
4. What states of matter is your body made of?

Making Connections

1. What state of matter is the cereal you can eat for breakfast?
2. What different states of matter are in your bathroom?
3. Why does ice melt?

Name ______________________________ Date ______________

Sharpen Your Skills

❶ If you put these words in alphabetical order, which word would come first?

❍ gas ❍ liquid
❍ solid ❍ matter

❷ Water can be changed into different **states** of matter.
What does the word "states" mean?

❍ places ❍ types
❍ countries ❍ piles

❸ What is the describing word (adjective) in this sentence?
Gases can be pushed into small spaces.

❍ gases ❍ spaces
❍ pushed ❍ small

❹ Which word best fits this sentence?
A liquid can change shape to ________ up glasses of different sizes.

❍ fill ❍ fulled
❍ full ❍ filled

❺ Which word would finish this analogy?
Table is to **solid** like **air** is to ______________.

❍ liquid ❍ solid
❍ matter ❍ gas

Name ______________________________ Date ______________

Get Logical

Callie went to the beach with her brother and her dad. They each discovered a different form of matter that they thought was interesting. Use the clues below to decide which state of matter each person discovered.

Clues

1. Callie's dad felt the air of the blowing breeze.
2. Callie loved to see the waves crashing on the rocks.
3. Callie's brother was too busy playing with his shovel to see the waves.

Solid			
Liquid			
Gas			
	Callie	Callie's brother	Callie's dad

Callie discovered a ______________________.

Callie's brother discovered a ______________________.

Callie's dad discovered a ______________________.

Matter

Which forms of matter take up space and have weight?

While children may brainstorm many answers based on the reading selection, this hands-on activity demonstrates how all forms of matter (solid, liquid, and gas) take up space and have weight.

Teacher Background Information

Some matter is made of just one kind of substance, or ingredient. Many forms of matter are made up of several substances, either combined together or just mixed together. It does not make any difference what kind of matter you have. All matter, whether it is big or small, takes up some space and weighs something. This idea can be difficult for young children to grasp, especially if you are talking about a gas. If the matter takes up space, then nothing else can be in that same space at the same time. If the matter is very small, it may not weigh much, but it will weigh something. In this experiment, water is used to test a liquid, air inside a cup and a balloon are used to test a gas, and paper is used to test a solid.

MATERIALS

(per group)

- ✔ container
- ✔ water
- ✔ piece of paper
- ✔ clear plastic cup
- ✔ tape (optional)
- ✔ balloon
- ✔ postal or kitchen scale

Procedure

1. Divide the class into groups of four to five children, and give each group a set of materials.
2. Ask children to take turns picking up the water container and to notice how heavy it feels while it is empty.
3. Have a child in each group fill the water container with water. Invite each child to pick up the container and notice how heavy it is now.
4. Have a child wad up the piece of paper and put it in the bottom of the cup.
5. Invite another child to turn the cup upside down. (The paper should NOT fall out. If it does, stick a loop of tape inside the cup to hold the paper better.)
6. Ask a child to push the upside-down cup into the water. Encourage children to observe what happens to the paper inside the cup.
7. Choose another child to weigh a deflated balloon on a small postal or kitchen scale and record how much it weighs.
8. Then, have another child blow up the balloon and weigh it on the scale. Ask children to notice how much the balloon weighs now.

Name ______________________________ Date ______________

Matter

Which forms of matter take up space and have weight?

Results and Conclusions

1. Was the water container heavier when it was empty or full? ________ Why?

____

2. Did the water take up space? ________

3. What happened to the paper inside the cup when it was pushed underwater?

____

4. Did the paper get wet? ________ Why or why not?

____

5. Did the empty balloon or the balloon with air weigh more? ________ Why?

____

6. List which forms of matter take up space and have weight.

____

Catch a Clue

What will we learn about in our reading today?

planets

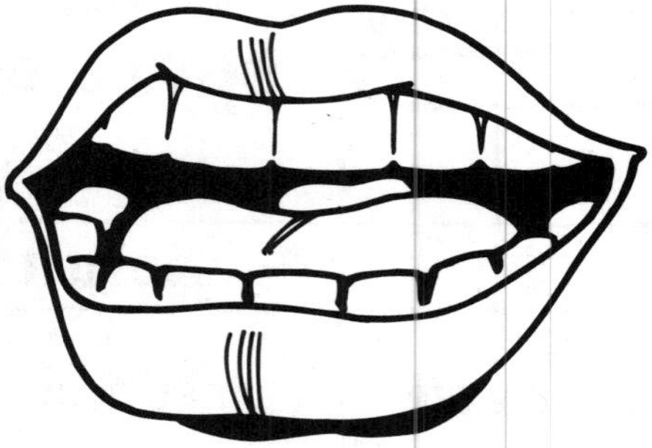

our teeth

simple machines

lights

Our Clues

1. **We use them every day.**
2. **They are not on our body.**
3. **They can move, cut, and build things.**

Concept Map

Facts we already know about **simple machines,** and the new facts we have learned

Word Warm-Up

Which words might you expect to find in a story about **simple machines?**

surface	shovel	inclined
wagon	pushing	seesaw
lift	sunshine	pizza cutter
building	furniture	plane

Simple Machines

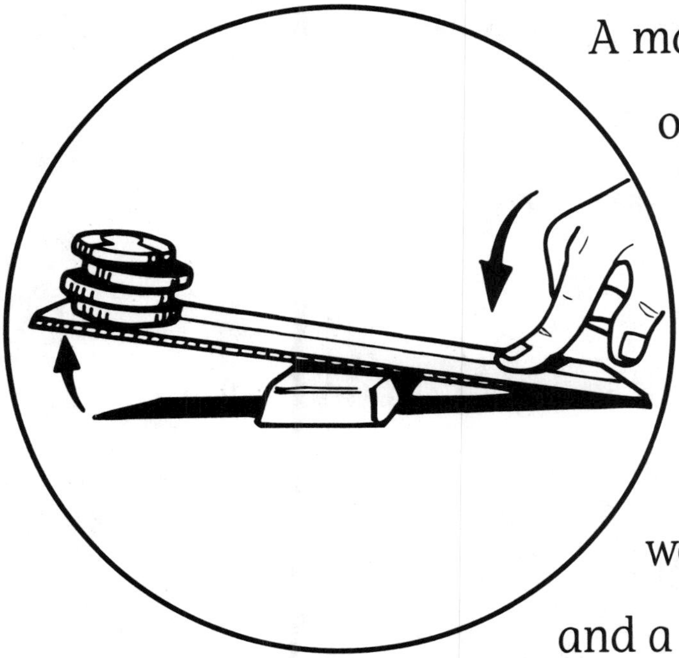

A machine is a tool that helps us with our work. All machines are made up of one or more simple machines. There are six kinds of simple machines. They are a lever, an inclined plane, a wedge, a screw, a wheel and axle, and a pulley.

A lever is a long rod or bar. Think of a seesaw. The long board of the seesaw is a lever. It is held steady, but it can move up and down. Spoons, shovels, and hammers can all be used as levers. Your pencil can be used as a lever, too!

An inclined plane, or ramp, is a flat surface that is at a slant. It is used to raise and lower things. A furniture mover will use an inclined plane to put a desk on a ramp to get it in the truck.

A wedge is two inclined planes put together. It is shaped like a triangle. The pointy end can be used to cut or split things. Or, it can hold them in place. A doorstop and the tip of a nail are wedges.

A screw is an inclined plane. It just goes around and around. There are many kinds of screws. Most of them hold things together.

Wheel and axle machines help to move things. Have you taken your pet for a ride in a wagon? If so, then you have used a wheel and axle. A bike, a pizza cutter, and a doorknob also use this simple machine.

A wheel with a groove in it can make a pulley. It has a cord that wraps around the wheel. It is used to help lift or move things. The flag at your school is raised with a pulley.

Now that you know the six kinds of simple machines, you can look for them. Look at the tools you use when you play and do work at home and school. They will use one or more of these six simple machines.

Comprehension Questions

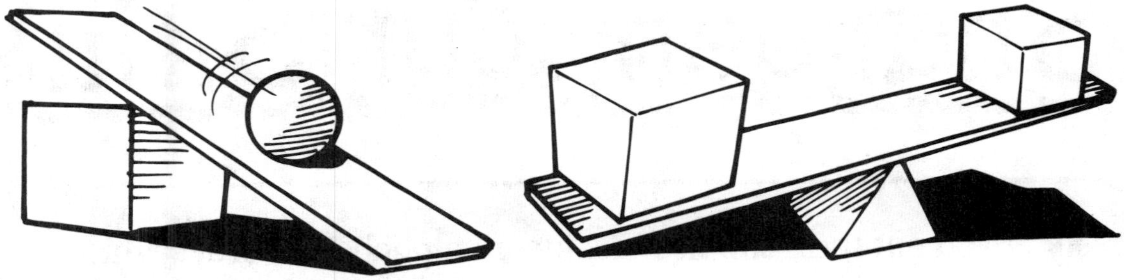

Literal Questions

1. What does a simple machine do?
2. What are the six different types of simple machines?
3. What kind of simple machine does a seesaw have?
4. What kind of simple machine is used to raise a flag?

Inferential Questions

1. Why do we need simple machines in our lives?
2. What kinds of simple machines make up a screwdriver?
3. What kind of simple machine would you use to open and close curtains on a window?
4. What kind of simple machine is a playground slide?

Making Connections

1. What simple machine would you like to make? Why?
2. Which two simple machines do you think are the most similar? Why?
3. In what ways do you use simple machines in your life?

Name ______________________________ Date ______________

Sharpen Your Skills

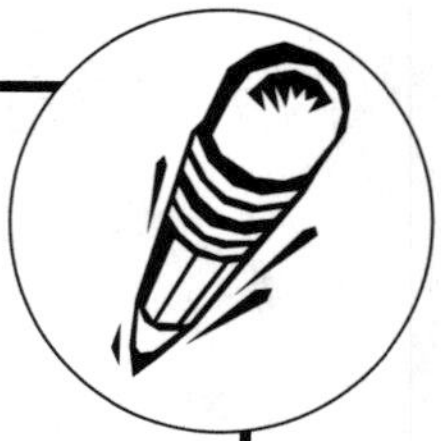

❶ If you put these simple machines in alphabetical order, which word would come last?

❍ pulley ❍ screw
❍ lever ❍ wedge

❷ Simple machines **aid** us by making our work easier.

What does the word "aid" mean?

❍ sick ❍ move
❍ help ❍ work

❸ Which word is a person, place, or thing (noun) in this sentence?

A lever can help you lift things up.

❍ lever ❍ lift
❍ help ❍ up

❹ Which word in the following sentence is made of two smaller words (compound word)?

If you dig up the flowers in a flowerpot, you will be using a simple machine.

❍ will ❍ simple machine
❍ dig ❍ flowerpot

❺ Which word would finish this analogy?

Lever is to **long rod** like **inclined plane** is to ________.

❍ bike ❍ screw
❍ spoon ❍ ramp

Name ______________________________ Date ______________

Get Logical

Daniel, Miguel, and Nina used simple machines to do their work over the weekend. Use the clues below to decide which simple machine each child used.

Clues

1. Miguel helped his dad push a shopping cart at the store.
2. Daniel helped his mom pry open the lid on a paint can.
3. Nina helped her sister push a box up a ramp.

Lever			
Wheel and Axle			
Inclined Plane			
	Daniel	Miguel	Nina

Daniel used the ______________________________.

Miguel used the ______________________________.

Nina used the ______________________________.

Simple Machines

How can simple machines help you do work more easily?

While children may brainstorm many answers based on the reading selection, this hands-on activity demonstrates how the placement of the fulcrum affects the lever's effectiveness to lift heavy objects.

Teacher Background Information

A lever is a rod, bar, or other long, hard object that is used to move things. For a lever to work, it must rest on a steady object but be able to move in different directions. The steady object that supports the lever is called the fulcrum. Sometimes the fulcrum is part of the lever itself like the top of tweezers where the two long arms are joined. Other times the fulcrum can be an object underneath the lever, like a crowbar resting on a rock to lift up a car. The fulcrum can be located anywhere along the lever. It may be between the weight and where you push, like it is with scissors, pliers, or a seesaw. The fulcrum can be on one end of the lever with the weight in the middle, like it is on a nutcracker, wheelbarrow, or bottle opener, while your force is exerted on the other end. Or, the fulcrum can be on one end of the lever with the weight on the other end and your push exerted in the middle, like it is on a broom, shovel, or tweezers. All levers can be used to lift or move a heavy load (weight). The position of the fulcrum influences how hard or easy it is to lift an object.

MATERIALS

(per group)

- ✔ Diagrams reproducible (page 113)
- ✔ masking tape
- ✔ small plastic container
- ✔ $1\frac{1}{2}$–2' (45.5–61 cm) flat piece of wood or strong particle board
- ✔ weights (e.g., rocks, metal washers)
- ✔ triangle-shaped block (for the fulcrum)

Procedure

1. Divide the class into groups of four to five children, and give each group a set of materials.
2. Ask a child in each group to securely tape the plastic container onto one end of the board.
3. Have another child fill the plastic container with the weights.
4. Invite another child to place the fulcrum (triangle block) under the lever board as shown in Diagram #1 on the Diagrams reproducible.
5. Tell one child to use his or her hand to push on the end of the board without the weight and notice how hard or easy it is to lift the weight. Invite every child to try this.
6. Ask another child to place the fulcrum under the lever board as shown in Diagram #2 and repeat step 5.
7. Invite another child in each group to place the fulcrum under the lever board as shown in Diagram #3 and repeat step 5.

Name ______________________ Date ______________

Simple Machines

How can simple machines help you do work more easily?

Diagrams

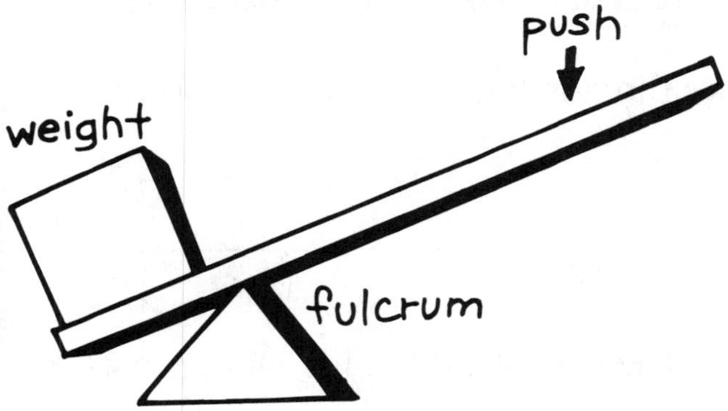

Diagram #1

Diagram #2

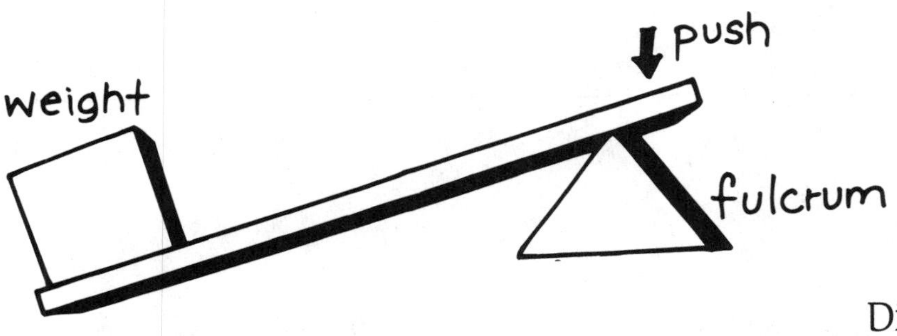

Diagram #3

Name ______________________ Date ____________

Simple Machines

How can simple machines help you do work more easily?

Results and Conclusions

1. Which diagram shows the hardest way to lift, Diagram #1, #2, or #3?

____

2. Which diagram shows the easiest way to lift, Diagram #1, #2, or #3?

____

3. Is a lever easier to use when the fulcrum is closer to or farther away from the weight to be lifted?

____

4. How can simple machines help you do work more easily?

____

Catch a Clue

What will we learn about in our reading today?

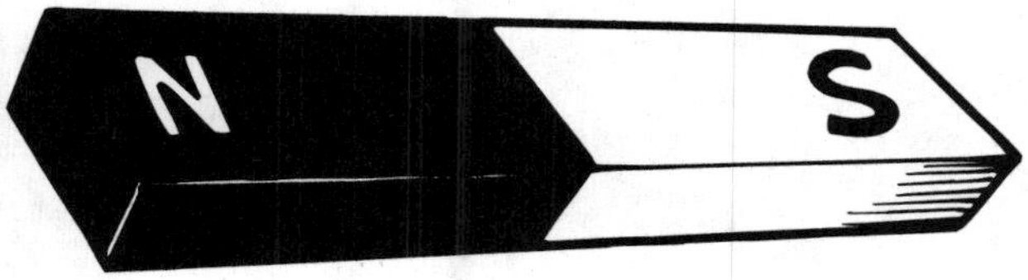

magnets

electricity

weather

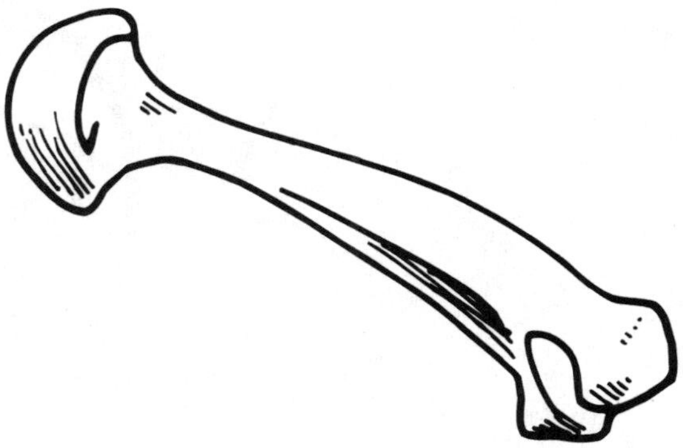

bones

Our Clues

1. **It involves things that become attached.**
2. **We will learn about north and south poles.**
3. **Your doorbell might have some.**

Concept Map

Facts we already know about **magnets,** and the new facts we have learned

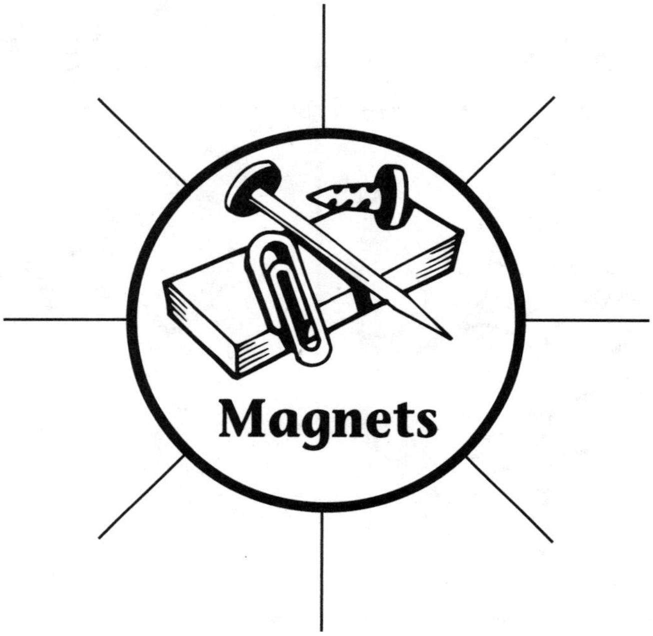

Word Warm-Up

Which words might you expect to find in a story about **magnets?**

trains	cobalt	stick
safety	materials	object
factories	water	south pole
energy	nail	north pole

Magnets

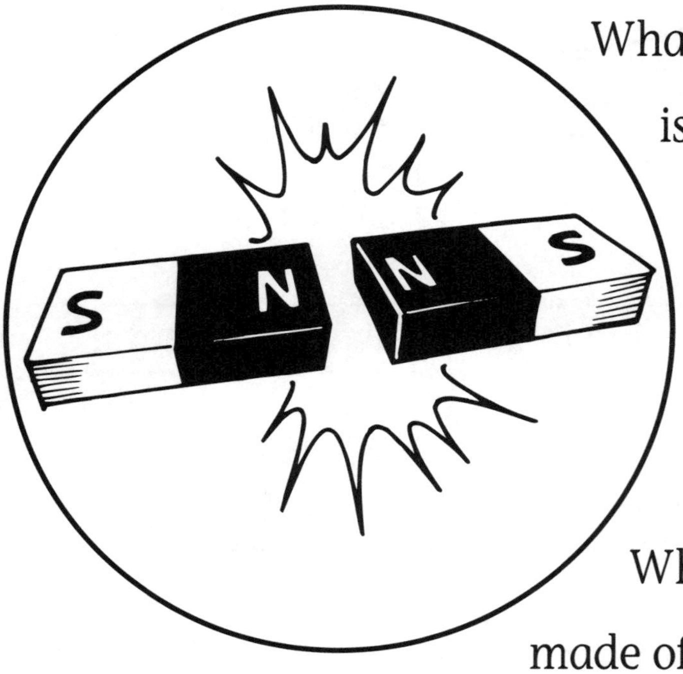

What is a magnet? It is an object that is made of nickel, iron, cobalt, or steel that sticks to other things. Magnets can stick to other magnets, too. They can also push away from other magnets.

Why are some things that are made of iron or steel not magnetic? A magnet made of iron can pick up things. A nail that is also made of iron cannot pick up things. Do you know why? There are small bits of iron in the magnet. They all face the same way. This lets them work together. It gives them the energy to pick up things. But, in the nail, the small bits of iron all face in different ways. They do not work together. They cannot pick up things.

You cannot see the energy of a magnet. It is all around the magnet. It is strongest at the ends. These are called the poles. All magnets have a north pole and a south pole. The north pole of one magnet will stick to the south pole of other magnets. When the north poles of two magnets are next to each other, they will push away from each other.

You can make some things act like a magnet. If you rub a pin on a magnet, that pin can pick up other pins. Try this at home to see how many pins you can pick up. This kind of magnet will not last long.

Magnets are used to help us in a lot of ways. They make your doorbell work and make some trains stay on their tracks! What kinds of magnets can you find? What are they used for?

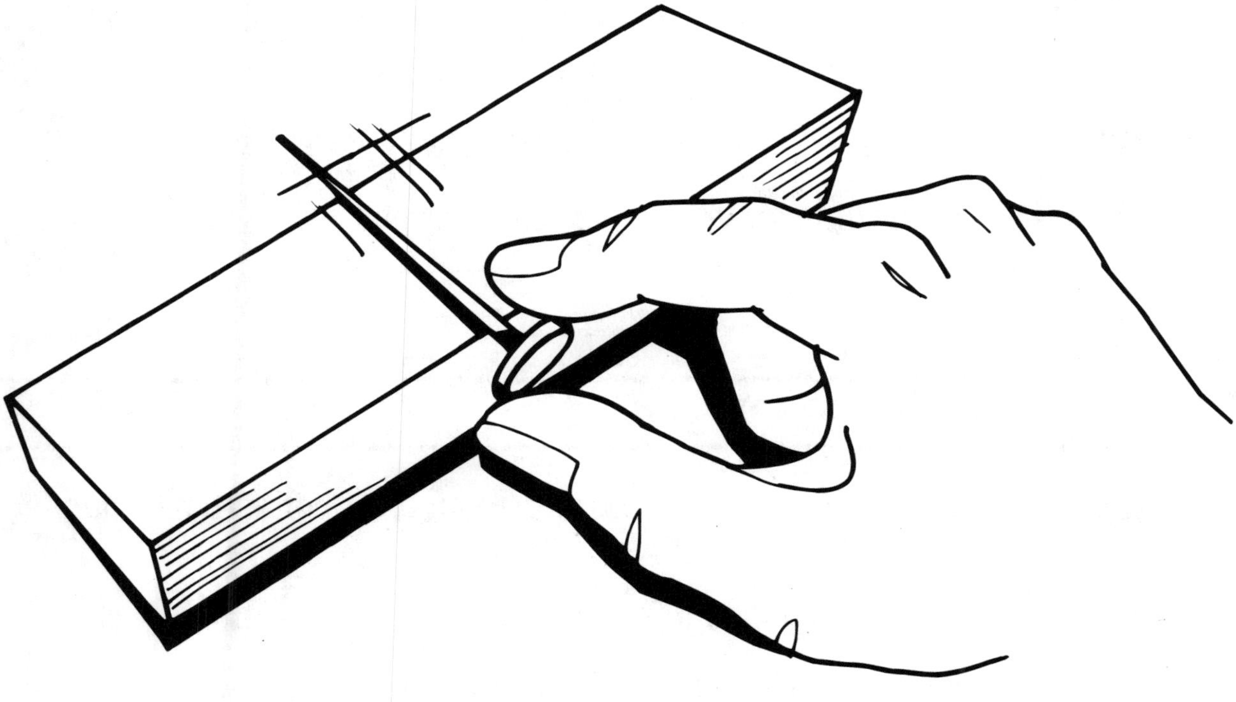

Comprehension Questions

Literal Questions

1. What is a magnet?
2. Can you see the energy around a magnet?
3. How can magnets be used to help us?
4. What are the four materials that can be magnetic?

Inferential Questions

1. Spoons are sometimes made out of stainless steel. Why aren't they magnets?
2. If you have two bar magnets, how can you make them stick together?
3. Why do you think a pin can pick up other pins after you rub it on a magnet?

Making Connections

1. What items can you find in the classroom or at home that a magnet would pick up?
2. What other ways do magnets help us in our daily lives?
3. What would you like to try to do with magnets?

Name ______________________________ Date ______________

Sharpen Your Skills

1 If you put these words in alphabetical order, which word would come third?

❍ nickel ❍ iron
❍ cobalt ❍ steel

2 If you want to make a pin magnetic, you need to **stroke** it with a magnet many times in the same direction.

What does the word "stroke" mean?

❍ heart attack ❍ rub
❍ poke ❍ stack

3 What is the action word (verb) in this sentence?

The north pole of one magnet pushes away the north pole of another magnet.

❍ north ❍ pole
❍ magnet ❍ pushes

4 Which word best fits this sentence?

An object is ________ if it can attract another object.

❍ magnet ❍ magnets
❍ magnetic ❍ magnetize

5 Which word would finish this analogy?

Fruit is to **sweet** like ____________ is to **magnetic.**

❍ salt ❍ steel
❍ wax ❍ wood

Name ______________________ Date ____________

Get Logical

Tamara, Carlos, and Miguel were at the Magnet Investigation Station. Use the clues below to decide what each child did.

Clues

1. Miguel's magnets pushed away from each other!
2. Tamara rubbed something with a magnet to make it magnetic.
3. Carlos made one magnet "stick" to another magnet.

	Tamara	Carlos	Miguel
Picked up 7 paper clips with only 1 paper clip			
Lined up the north pole of one magnet with the north pole of another magnet			
Lined up the north pole of one magnet with the south pole of another magnet			

Tamara ______________________.

Carlos ______________________.

Miguel ______________________.

Magnets

What kinds of objects will a magnet pick up?

While children may brainstorm many answers based on the reading selection, this hands-on activity demonstrates that a magnet is attracted to objects made of iron, steel, nickel, and cobalt.

Teacher Background Information

Magnets are objects that will pick up or attract other objects made out of iron, steel, nickel, or cobalt. Young children often mistakenly think magnets will pick up any kind of metal. Magnets themselves can only be made out of these same magnetic materials. The invisible energy of a magnet, called the magnetic field, surrounds the magnet and is strongest at the ends, called poles. Two magnets placed together will attract each other if their poles are different (N–S). They will repel each other if the poles are the same (N–N). The invisible energy of a magnet can pass through other nonmagnetic objects. The closer the object is to the magnet, the more strongly it will be attracted.

MATERIALS

(per group)

- ✔ Magnet Data Chart reproducible (page 124)
- ✔ 2 bar magnets
- ✔ pin
- ✔ plastic button
- ✔ rubber eraser
- ✔ paper clip
- ✔ craft stick
- ✔ penny
- ✔ aluminum foil
- ✔ nail

Procedure

1. Divide the class into groups of four to five children, and give each group a set of materials.
2. Ask all children to look at the objects and separate them into two piles—one for things they think a magnet will pick up and one for things they think a magnet will not pick up. Have children check off the prediction boxes on their Magnet Data Chart reproducible according to their two piles.
3. Invite all children to test each object separately by touching it with a magnet to see if the magnet will pick it up.
4. Have children record their observations on their reproducible.
5. Ask a child to place the two bar magnets next to each other on the table and observe what happens.
6. Invite children to turn one magnet around in the opposite direction, bring the magnets close together again, and observe what happens.

Name ________________________ Date ____________

Magnets

What kinds of objects will a magnet pick up?

Magnet Data Chart

Object Tested	Predict—Yes	Predict—No	Test—Yes	Test—No
Pin				
Plastic button				
Rubber eraser				
Paper clip				
Craft stick				
Penny				
Aluminum foil				
Nail				

Name ______________________ Date ____________

Magnets

What kinds of objects will a magnet pick up?

Results and Conclusions

1. What is something new you learned about magnets?

____

2. Did the two bar magnets stick to each other when you put them together?

____

Why or why not?

____

3. What happened when you put the two bar magnets together in a different way?

____

4. What kinds of objects will a magnet pick up?

____

Catch a Clue

What will we learn about in our reading today?

shadows

cows

pancakes

flowers

❶ They are not living things.

❷ You can use your hands to form them.

❸ They involve light.

Concept Map

Facts we already know about **shadows,** and the new facts we have learned

Word Warm-Up

Which words might you expect to find in a story about **shadows?**

buildings	afternoon	light
direction	wonder	frosted
change	minerals	waves
dark	object	curtains

Shadows

Each year on February 2nd, we wait to see if the groundhog will see its shadow. Have you seen your shadow? Where did it come from?

When you stand outside on a sunny day, your body blocks some of the light from hitting the ground. Light waves travel in a straight line. They cannot bend around you. Your shadow is the dark area in the shape of your body you see on the ground.

Not all objects block light waves. Light can pass through some things. Air, water, and glass are clear and do not block the light. Other objects let some light pass through, but you cannot clearly see what is on the other side. Waxed paper, frosted glass, and some shower curtains let some light through. Some things do not let any light through. Buildings, cars, and people do not let any light through. You cannot see through them. They make shadows.

Did you know that on a sunny day your shadow can change sizes? Your shadow will look very short or really tall as the sun moves across the sky in the day. When the sun is right over your head, you do not block much light. So, you will not see a big shadow of yourself. You can make a longer shadow early in the morning and late in the afternoon. This is because the sun is low in the sky. Can you see your shadow inside the classroom? Most of the time, you do not make shadows inside a room or at night. There is not a lot of light for your body to block.

Go outside at different times on a sunny day. Watch how your shadow grows or shrinks in the day. Look at where the sun is each time. Your shadow will be on the side away from the sun because you block the light. If you run fast enough, do you think you can get away from your shadow? Try it and see!

Comprehension Questions

Literal Questions

1. What makes a shadow?
2. When is a shadow short? When is it long?
3. When will you most likely not see a shadow at all?
4. What can make a shadow?

Inferential Questions

1. How will your shadow change from the morning to the middle of the day?
2. Why can't you make your shadow go away?
3. Where can you see a shadow?
4. What can you use to make shadows at night?

Making Connections

1. What funny shadow animals can you make?
2. When is your shadow the longest?
3. Go outside. What shadows do you see?

Name ______________________ Date ______________

Sharpen Your Skills

1. If you put these words in alphabetical order, which word would come last?

   ❍ light ❍ shadows
   ❍ sky ❍ dark

2. In the middle of the day, your shadow will **vanish** from sight. What does the word "vanish" mean?

   ❍ appear ❍ disappear
   ❍ shine ❍ smile

3. What is the action word (verb) in this sentence?
   You can make shadows outside.

   ❍ outside ❍ can
   ❍ make ❍ shadows

4. What is the contraction for **cannot** in this sentence?
   You can't see your shadow at night since it isn't light.

   ❍ can't ❍ isn't
   ❍ see ❍ since

5. Which word would finish this analogy?
   Morning is to **night** like **light** is to ____________.

   ❍ bright ❍ shiny
   ❍ dark ❍ damp

Name ______________________ Date ____________

Get Logical

Alex, Barry, and Kobe each went outside to see his shadow at a different time of the day. Use the clues below to decide when each boy saw his shadow.

Clues

1. Barry was at school, but he could not see his shadow at all.
2. Kobe's shadow was long.
3. Alex could not see any shadows outside.

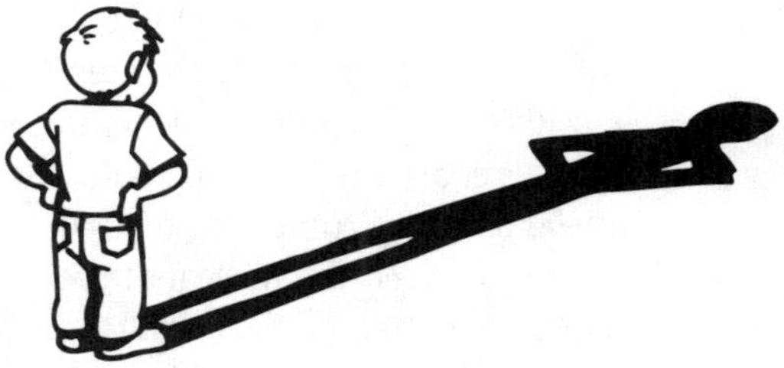

8:00 a.m.			
12:00 noon			
10:00 p.m.			
	Alex	Barry	Kobe

Alex looked for his shadow at ______________.

Barry looked for his shadow at ______________.

Kobe looked for his shadow at ______________.

Shadows

How can you record the size and shape of a shadow?

While children may brainstorm many answers based on the reading selection, this hands-on activity demonstrates how to "take a picture" of a shadow using special blueprint paper.

Teacher Background Information

The experiment requires blueprint paper, which is available (often free to teachers) at blueprint shops or architectural offices. Look up the nearest shop in the yellow pages. The paper comes in large sheets, which can easily be cut into small 4" x 6" (10 cm x 15 cm) pieces for children. One side has a yellow emulsion on it that is sensitive to light. Store the paper in a dark bag or envelope until you are ready to use it. Prepare the "developer jars" ahead of time. Crumple up a piece of waxed paper, and place it at the bottom of each group's jar. Pour in about 1" (2.5 cm) of ammonia, and then immediately close the jar. (Ammonia fumes can hurt your eyes and nose.) This will be the developer jar. Do this experiment in the early morning or afternoon on a sunny day to get the best "shadow pictures." Everywhere the light is blocked, a blue color will appear when the picture is developed. You will need several parent helpers for this experiment.

MATERIALS

(per child)

- ✔ small piece of slow-acting blueprint paper
- ✔ paper plate
- ✔ glue
- ✔ construction paper

(per group)

- ✔ medium-sized wide-mouthed jar with lid
- ✔ waxed paper
- ✔ a bottle of ammonia
- ✔ assorted small items (e.g., toy figures, animals, buttons, keys, letters)

Procedure

1. Divide the class into groups of four to five children, assign a parent helper to each group, and give each group a set of materials.
2. Have each child place a piece of blueprint paper (yellow side up) in the middle of his or her paper plate. Ask each child to arrange a few small objects or toys standing on his or her paper.
3. Invite children to take their plate outside into the sun. Notice where the sun is, and ask children to observe the shadows their objects make on the yellow paper.
4. Have children wait in the sun for at least 30 seconds and watch their yellow paper turn to white in the sunlight. Tell children they have just "taken" a picture.
5. Take the class back to the classroom, and have them remove all objects from their paper.
6. Have the parent helper open the developer jar, insert a child's paper, and then quickly close the jar. (The paper should not touch the liquid in the bottom of the jar.)
7. Encourage children to watch as each shadow picture develops. (It should take 1–2 minutes.)
8. Have the parent helper remove the paper from the jar, and then repeat steps 6–8 until every child's picture has been developed.
9. Invite children to glue their shadow picture onto a piece of construction paper. Ask children to write their name and the title *Shadow Pictures* at the top.

Name ______________________ Date ____________

Shadows

How can you record the size and shape of a shadow?

Results and Conclusions

1. What objects did you use to make shadows?

____

2. Was the sun low in the sky or high in the sky when you went outside to "take" your picture?

____

3. What did you learn from this experiment?

____

4. How can you record the size and shape of a shadow?

____